To Receive Your FREE GIFT

$100K Launch Video Series

6 Figure Roadmap Guide &

to learn more information,

visit the website at

<u>www.100KOutofCollege.com</u>

Dedication

To our parents, Patricia Quinlan, James Quinlan and Debbie Weir, who raised us right, showed us love, taught us well and always supported us in our journey to pursue our dreams. Without you we wouldn't be where we are today and this book would not be possible. To that we say thank you — thanks for everything.

Epigraph

Far and away the best prize that life offers is the chance to work hard at work worth doing.

—Theodore Roosevelt
26th President of the United States

When you do the common things in life in an uncommon way, you will command the attention of the world.

—George Washington Carver
American botanist & inventor

A pessimist sees the difficulty in every opportunity; an optimist sees the opportunity in every difficulty.

—Winston Churchill
Prime Minister of the United Kingdom, artist & writer

Contents

How to Make

$100K

Out of College

Discover the 6 Simple Insider Secrets

to Making 6 Figures a Year

Doing What You Love

Kevin Quinlan • Wes Rowlands

Traditional education is based on facts and figures and passing tests — not on a comprehension of the material and its application to your life.

—Will Smith
American actor, producer, rapper & songwriter

Preface

How to Make $100K Out of College is a book about doing just that — showing you how to make a six-figure income out of college. We define "out of college" as reaching this milestone before the age of 30, if not years sooner. To be clear, this is not a "get rich quick" scheme. In fact, we acknowledge that the road to earning a high income will likely take you several years of planning and hard work, but we'll share everything we can to expedite the process for you. While it's important for you understand that anything valuable takes time and effort, it's equally as important to cut out any inefficiencies to reach your goal – in this case, making $100K or more.

In this book you will learn our six "insider secrets" based on years of experience of how PROPER PLANNING AND STRATEGIC THINKING can get you there rather than simply relying on luck — which we believe is a function of intentional action. To put it another way, you create your own good fortune by performing the work and putting yourself in position to be successful. We know because we have been there ourselves. We have held jobs in the marketplace that have earned these salaries. We simply want to share what we have learned to get you there soon after you walk down the aisle with your cap and gown at graduation.

We chose to write a book on this particular topic because the content of "HOW" TO DO THIS IS NOT BEING TAUGHT IN SCHOOLS and you will not find another book teaching you the key secrets of how to get there. For today's younger generation, it's particularly important to learn how to make money so that you can live your very own version of the American Dream. Students coming out of college need to hear from a variety of people, but it's especially helpful to hear from recent graduates who are role models in the working world.

All content in this book is taken directly from hand selected real-world professionals who became successful in a variety of industries. They will give you an insider peek at their journeys of how they made it to $100K at an early age. They will teach you key learning points, insights and advice that will prove to be essential to your success. These interviews are full disclosure. Because of the relationships in place with those being interviewed, there are no politically correct answers. For privacy purposes, we have changed their names but there is no censorship. You will not learn this in a classroom — it does not get any more real.

As you will learn in this book, rewards are not only possible…they are SPECIFICALLY ACHIEVABLE FOR YOU AND FOR ALL PEOPLE WHO ARE WILLING TO PUT IN THE WORK!

To be upfront, we issue a few words of transparency; climbing the ladder to $100K will be more attainable in certain careers much sooner than others. We will not bullshit you – we'd much rather deal with reality. As an example, if you select a job as a teacher (a position one of the authors once held) or government employee, it may — and likely will — take years longer to achieve high levels of financial success. In fact, some careers will simply never pay even close to $100,000 per year. And that's completely fine if that's what you want to do. We just want to help you be cognizant of what you are signing up for. You definitely don't want to graduate with $150,000 in student loans with a career that's only going to be paying you $30,000 a year for the next ten years!

To be fair, if your passion is teaching (a typically low paying occupation), it doesn't mean you are condemning yourself to a life of mediocre compensation – you just may have to get a bit more creative to earn a higher level of income. For instance, you may consider starting your own business teaching online, or writing and selling your own books, or pursuing other entrepreneurial opportunities in your passion area to earn more money. Point is, while it's important to understand the typical earnings spectrum of your desired industry, there are no pre-defined limits that YOU are subject to.

To help provide you with some perspective on different career paths, see the Appendices at the back of the book for top paying industries and entry-level jobs.

So how should you use this book? Each of you should read the book, take notes and review them often. You will find revisiting them for even for a few minutes every week to be a much more valuable use of your time than perfecting your latest duck face selfie on Snapchat or trying to find the next creature in *Pokémon Go.* Then apply the secrets and advice you learned to be successful. What we can guarantee you is if you take the principles and guidance offered in this book and APPLY THEM TO YOUR OWN WORK, YOU WILL INCREASE YOUR WORTH IN THE MARKETPLACE AND BE REWARDED FOR IT.

The first half of this text will teach you the essential principles to grow a career that earns you $100,000 per year. In these chapters we will share with you the six insider secrets to making six figures a year, early in your career. In the second half, we share with you the word-for-word advice directly from people WHO ARE ALREADY MAKING OVER $100K. They will teach you step by step what they did to get where they are and how you can do it too IF YOU PUT IN THE WORK.

During these interviews, we will weigh in with our own analysis called *"Brain Bucks"* to highlight key takeaways and reoccurring themes that would be of great value to use for your career.

We wish you luck on your career journey but first a few words on what it is that makes earning $100K a key goal for so many people....

Is freedom anything else than the right to live as we wish? Nothing else.

—Epictetus
Greek philosopher

Introduction

Ah, that magic number. $100,000. One-hundred. Thousand. Dollars. $100K. 100 G's. I remember when playing hide-and-go-seek as a kid, having to close my eyes and count to 100 before I could begin searching for my friends (all two of them). It seemed like I was counting for 20 minutes, with 100 being such a large number, and it certainly was a long way from zero. I recall getting excited with growing anticipation as I counted into the 80s, and even more into the 90s. With each passing number, "91....92....93...94," my voice became increasingly excited, louder and faster as I got closer to that monumental number. At last I would shout, "100 — ready or not, here I come!" Little did I know that my friends weren't hiding but still running, probably to the nearest Wawa convenience store.

So, what is it about that number, $100K? Is it all the zeros? That comma in the middle that equally divides the six digits? The sound the syllables make? It does have a nice ring to it, doesn't it? Or that briefcase full of crisp $100 bills that we envision? What about the things we can do with those dollars — the things we can buy and the experiences we can have?

Game shows including *The Price Is Right, Wheel of Fortune* and *Who Wants to be a Millionaire* have millions of viewers tuning in to each show to see contestants having a chance to change their lives and fortunes by playing a pricing game, getting to the bonus round or answering several consecutive questions correctly to win large amounts of money, with a top prize usually being that monumental $100,000 figure. Heck, there's even a candy bar called *100 Grand*, which includes chewy caramel, milk chocolate and crisped rice — a very satisfying combination for some. The bar's slogan is *"That's rich."* Kind of fitting that many people associate someone who makes more than "100 grand" each year to be rich.

In the working world, for some, this monetary figure is a symbol (or number rather) of success, "good" or "great" money and someone who is considered to be "doing really well." I think for most people, it symbolizes freedom.

Financial freedom, that is — freedom to buy, freedom to go and freedom to do. Freedom to do whatever you please and enjoy the riches and experiences that life has to offer. And this freedom can also make us feel more powerful too.

For me, a certain date sticks out in mind. November 5, 2014 — the day my salary increased to $100K. I remember it like yesterday. For months I had been performing the work of the manager above me AND PROVIDING VALUE BEFORE ASKING FOR A PAY INCREASE. Finally, when the time was right, I requested a bump in salary and got it! Not only did I receive what I asked for, my employer gave me more — pushing me over the $100,000 mark! It felt pretty damn good. It felt like I "made it." I don't tell you this to brag but to simply show an example of career progression.

After allowing it to sink in, I asked myself, "How did I get here?" I took a moment to reflect on my entire career to see how I arrived at this figure:

- Fourteen years prior, I was making $5.25 per hour at my first job as a sales associate and cashier at a sneaker and apparel store called The Athlete's Foot at the local mall. This was during the year 2000 and I was a freshman in high school when I started.

- Nine years prior, I was making $10 per hour at a beach bar nightclub providing security and checking IDs. I hated this job and the hours that came with it but stuck it out for the summer. Knowing the bar and nightlife industry wasn't for me helped drive me to find other areas I was interested in such as business and education.

- Seven years prior, I held a paid internship during my senior year of college making $120 monthly for about 5 hours of work per week. The money wasn't great nor important but THE INTERNSHIP WAS THE REAL CURRENCY. I can tell you the biggest value here that still pays off for me to this day was the key EXPERIENCE AND CREDIBILITY I could take with me when interviewing for entry-level jobs during my senior year of college. It is the ONLY REASON why I was able to secure my first job before starting my final semester of college. This book goes into internships in great depth including strategies for obtaining them in Chapter 2 and resurfaces again with the $100K earners we interviewed.

- Six years prior, I had begun my post-college career as a business analyst making $48,000 per year a few miles outside of Washington, D.C. — again largely in part to the internship I held during my senior year.
- Four years prior, I was making $57,000 per year as a consultant.
- Two years prior, I began working independently as a consultant conducting market research for my former employer. I became highly skilled and efficient in performing this type of specialized work.
    - I started at $30 an hour.
    - Within two years I had gone from $30 ($62,400) to $37 ($76,990) to $42 an hour ($87,360).
    - And now here I was finally making $50 an hour, which came out to be $104,000 for the year.
- I also had a tremendous work-life balance that gave me the flexibility to earn my master's degree in my passion area, start my own business and write this book. Most importantly, I was very much enjoying the work I was performing.

So how the hell did I get from $62,400 to $104,000, increasing my pay by more than $41,000 dollars or by 66% in just two years' time? How do I explain reaching this milestone and what do I attribute it to?

Deep down inside, I know this is an end result that has been achieved by following our recipe of six insider secrets, which we'll share with you over the next several chapters. First and foremost, I started by following my passions (which is a topic we dive into in Chapter 1). First, my passion of pursuing a career in business and later my passion in education, teaching business and technology courses to students. I began both of these careers by going through valuable internship experiences. Being a life-long learner, I was always interested in acquiring new skills (more on learning new skills in Chapter 6) and ways of thinking. I've always kept and applied the strong interpersonal and communication skills my parents instilled within me to create strong relationships (the focus of Chapter 4) to advance my career. Unfortunately, these skills are not taught nor acquired during most student's formal education growing up. They helped me stand out from my competition.

The other key component was the great internship on my résumé. I will tell you that I am no genius. I went to a very good four-year university, but it certainly wasn't Ivy League. But I was a very hard worker (you will learn more about hard work in Chapter 3) and where I have been most successful in working hard, I had a passion for the work I was performing. And I had mentors along the way (more about the value of mentors in Chapter 5).

We could go into our entire careers of how applying these foundational secrets ultimately catapulted us to cross the $100K mark in salary. But by now you get the point. And besides, this book is not all about us.

This book is about several extraordinary individuals who have demonstrated a strong work ethic and higher level thinking, and realized their potential in the marketplace early in their careers. Their paths, occupations and journeys are different. Several of them share similar strategies that overlap with our insider secrets, providing added proof that this stuff works. They have one commonality — they all found a way to make $100K *or more* out of college while in their mid-to-late 20s. Wouldn't you like to increase your value in the marketplace and be rewarded for it as they have? The good news is YOU CAN! ALL YOU HAVE TO DO IS READ THIS BOOK — ALL OF THE LESSONS AND INTERVIEWS, THEN GO OUT AND TAKE ACTION.

Most books and the lessons within them are of but little value. Their real value lies not in their printed pages but in the potential action they may produce in the reader. THAT'S YOU! Your earning power and potential are in your own hands, at your fingertips. It will then be up to you to create your own story — your own journey of how to get there. So if you're on board, let's begin and learn the six insider secrets to making $100K out of college.

Chapter 1: Secret #1
It Starts with a Pa$$ion

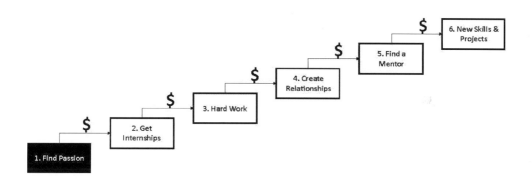

People say you have to have a lot of passion for what you're doing and it's totally true. And the reason is because it's so hard that if you don't, any rational person would give up. It's really hard. And you have to do it over a sustained period of time. So if you don't love it, if you're not having fun doing it, you don't really love it, you're going to give up. And that's what happens to most people, actually. If you really look at the ones that ended up, you know, being successful' in the eyes of society and the ones that didn't, oftentimes, it's the ones [who] were successful, loved what they did so they could persevere, you know, when it got really tough. And the ones that didn't love it quit because they're sane, right? Who would want to put up with this stuff if you don't love it?

So it's a lot of hard work and it's a lot of worrying constantly, and if you don't love it, you're going to fail. So you've got to love it and you've got to have passion, and I think that's the high-order bit.

—Steve Jobs
Co-founder, Chairman & CEO of Apple

The featured quote on the previous page is from one of the most brilliant men our world has seen in both innovation and business. It was Steve Jobs' take on passion. So what is it and what do we mean when we talk about it? If you look up the definition of "passion" in any dictionary, you will find something like the following:

> *A strong feeling of enthusiasm or excitement for something or about doing something.*

Some people think talking about passion and going after your passion is corny. Don't listen to those people — period. It is likely that they have not yet found or made the decision to work in their own passion, as they would surely understand if they had.

Career unhappiness and uncertainty are not fun places. It has been studied and reported that the majority of Americans are unhappy at work. We've experienced it ourselves but did not let it consume us for a long period of time and NEITHER SHOULD YOU. We took action, made career moves, sometimes finding new careers, and you will read about several others who have as well. Yet the majority of people wake up every day and go through the motions of "trying to get through another day." Some call it the "daily grind."

Those same people get excited and even draw mental pictures of camels in their mind as they celebrate "Hump Day" because for many, Wednesday signals the working week is more than halfway over. Those same people seem to be happier on Friday than on Tuesday. Why is that? Perhaps they always have some awesome plans for the weekend, but my guess is the bigger reason (and part of the problem) is because the end of the working day on Friday is the furthest point from starting another working week at the job they despise come Monday morning. Yes, that is when that inevitable clock before "grinding out another week" or "earning a paycheck" is at its highest. I was once one of those people. Our challenge for you is to NOT become one of those people.

I'll share with you a short story. Several years ago, I was offered a position that seemed like a great opportunity. I took a leap of faith and jumped at it. It didn't take long (about an entire two weeks) to realize that the position was not a good fit for me — in fact it was an awful fit. I liked the people on the team, but I LITERALLY HATED WHAT I WAS DOING! I FELT HORRIBLE WHEN I GOT HOME FROM WORK AND WHEN I WOKE UP EACH MORNING. SIMPLY PUT, I DREADED THE JOB.

So I did the only rational thing somebody in that scenario should do — I quit after 10 weeks. Given the job market with the conditions of the economy at the time (2012), it wasn't the most popular decision — in fact some people thought I was crazy. But I HAD A PLAN to pursue a new dream of earning a master's degree to become a teacher. Long story short, despite everyone telling me my "dream" was crazy-talk, within a few weeks, through hard work and precise action, I applied and got accepted into the exact master's program I had set out for. The only problem — I couldn't pay the bills. However, it's funny the way the world works sometimes when you know what you want and demand it to come true. Things have a way of working out. Without boring you with all of the details, I was able to land a job on the EXACT TERMS I WANTED, and it paid great money working part-time to fulfill my full-time dream.

Here's how I did it:

I needed income, so I had to get creative. I knew that my former employer frequently hires contractors. Combine that with the fact I had built great relationships and excelled from a performance standpoint ... so I decided to call my former employer and request to work in my old role, only this time as a contracted employee. Both sides could reap benefits. My employer knew I already had the skillset and wouldn't have to re-train me. While for myself, I was able to pursue my educational goals and continue to stay in the workforce and advance my career. For me, being creative meant identifying the resources I had at my disposal, putting the pieces together and PICKING UP THE PHONE AND ASKING!

Some of you may not have the same set-up of becoming a contracted employee for a company you previously worked for, but that doesn't give you an excuse. YOU HAVE THE SAME ABILITY TO GET CREATIVE IF THINGS AREN'T GOING AS PLANNED. There are plenty of opportunities available to you in today's world where you can find ways to make income on a part-time or hourly basis. For example, if you need to get by to make ends meet, sign up to drive for Uber or Lyft. If driving isn't your thing, join a freelance labor site like TaskRabbit so you can get paid money to perform tasks including cleaning, heavy lifting or putting together IKEA furniture. If you have some experience with more refined skills such as writing, customer service or working with data analytics, then try Upwork. Upwork is a global freelancing platform where businesses and independent professionals connect and collaborate remotely. In other words — you can perform the majority of these jobs from the comfort of your home where you won't waste time and money commuting to an office.

IT IS NEVER TOO LATE TO LEARN AND DO SOMETHING NEW if you have a curiosity for it with a profound passion on your side. So we know what you're now thinking and asking yourself: How do I find my passion? How do I ensure I am doing great work in my passion? If I'm not and am currently doing something else, where do I start over, and how do I get there?

Step 1: Learn your personality, learn about yourself. The answer of where to start is rather simple and may surprise you. Take a career assessment and analyze the results. Then EXPLORE THOSE RESULTS by taking the time (aka hours) to learn about matching careers! We know, you've probably heard all this before and it isn't your first go-around in taking a Myer-Briggs test. However, what we would ask you to consider is how *seriously* did you take it? How many *hours* did you spend on it?

I know I am guilty of not taking it seriously the first time. My first career assessment was during my junior year in high school. My #1 career choice based on the answers I provided was … tobacco grower! Now I don't mean any disrespect to all of the tobacco growers out there, but I know I was not put on this earth to do anything related to farming or growing tobacco. Hell, I don't even use tobacco-based products. That's an extreme example, but the deeper question to ask yourself is HOW MUCH EFFORT, TIME AND RESEARCH DID YOU PUT INTO GOING OVER THE RESULTS? Years later, I now see the value these assessments offer if taken seriously with the right approach — the same approach I should have used the first time. Without it, you are destined for a career of complacency and unhappiness making it harder for you to make the big bucks.

Step 2: Establish Your "S.E.T. Point." Once your career assessment is complete, let's take it to the next level by looking at what we call the "**S.E.T. Point.**" That is, what S̲kills, E̲nvironment and T̲opics would you prefer in your ideal workplace? For example, do you like to work with numbers? Write journal entries? Teach in front of a class? Number crunching, writing and teaching would all be illustrations of different **SKILLS** used in the workplace.

The next question to ask yourself is what E̲nvironment do you enjoy working in? Would you like working on the floor of the stock exchange where everything is super-fast paced? How about in a research laboratory where you can hear a pin drop? Do you want flexible hours or a fixed schedule? Would you prefer a hands-on boss who communicates with you multiple times a day or a boss who leaves you to your work and only wants to touch base at infrequent project milestones? All of these would be examples of **ENVIRONMENT** factors that are specific to the company and/or even the department where you will be working.

The final question is what are the T̲opics that interest you? Are you a huge sports fan? Do you like the fashion industry? Obsessed with cars? These all represent **TOPICS** that can be translated into your career. There are so many job outlets for every *topic* of interest. For example, if you are a huge football fan, you could go work for the NFL, as they hire accountants, lawyers, marketers, and on and on. Let's say you are into cosmetics — you could go work for Estee Lauder, a huge manufacturer of skin-care products that employs people for all types of occupations.

Let's look at an example of someone we know who established their *S.E.T. Point* and in return for doing so landed a career he is passionate about. A few years ago our friend was hired as the assistant basketball coach to an Ivy League basketball team. He thought this would be the best gig in the world since he loved coaching (**Skills**) and was completely head-over-heels for basketball (**Topic**), but he found himself completely miserable after just months of starting out because he hated how the head coach treated the rest of the staff. To clarify, he couldn't stand the **Environment** of that particular job. So what did he do? Rather than just quitting and starting a completely new profession, he recognized all he had to do was change the environment by going to work for another team. He has since made that change, got hired on a new team and has landed his dream job!

Remember, this is YOUR CAREER we're talking about! The very career that will determine your livelihood of how you provide for yourself and others. It's true that most people spend more time in their work environments and with co-workers than their families, so we cannot overstate the IMPORTANCE OF GETTING THIS RIGHT. Some of the great career assessments may cost you money. That's fine. ALWAYS INVEST IN YOURSELF. Sometimes that means with money, continuing education or time. This is an investment in yourself, one of the most important ones you will make in your lifetime.

I'll close this chapter by sharing a story that revisits the key point of finding your passion. I've been very fortunate to meet many interesting people in my life. People from different backgrounds, different places and different careers. A couple of them stand out from the rest. I once met an amazing woman from the Philadelphia area who, at a very young age, became a manager at an upscale restaurant owned by one of the most successful restaurateurs in the country.

For those of you who may be unfamiliar, this is an extremely challenging industry. To survive and excel within hospitality, you better be damn good in working with different people and a highly skilled communicator (skills we addressed earlier that are declining amongst the masses) to be an effective manager and leader. Those in the industry who love it would relish the opportunity to work for this owner. Let me put it to you this way, when one of his restaurants has a job opening for a manager position, hundreds of applicants compete for the opportunity.

Realizing how early she was in her career having only been a few years removed from college, I asked her how she got the job. She looked me in the eye and told me how working in this industry was her passion! She had the most radiant smile as she shared her story with me. Do you smile when telling people what you do for a living? Perhaps it's because you do not love your job as much as she loves hers. She went on to share that her passion came across enthusiastically and confidently during the rounds of job interviews. She was very direct in her answers. It was evident. It was authentic. It was clear to the company she was the right choice despite her young age compared to her more experienced competitors. It was clear to me as well. It comes as no surprise that her passion still burns for her industry and work today — she has since been promoted to manager of one of the most popular restaurants in the city.

Lesson learned — PASSION WINS. IT ALWAYS DOES AND IT ALWAYS WILL.

Chapter 2: Secret #2
Building Your Foundation
with Internhip

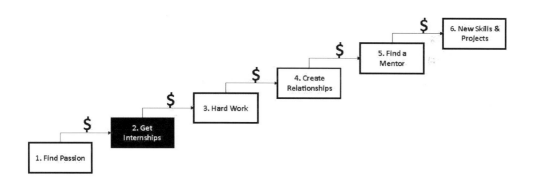

You miss 100% of the shots you don't take.

—Wayne Gretzky
Former professional Hall of Fame ice hockey player

While a whole book could be written on internships, we want to make sure to give you a quick action guide to using internships as your foundation for launching a successful career. That said, in this chapter we will teach you first and foremost why internships are more important than ever. You will then learn HOW TO GET YOUR FIRST INTERNSHIP, even if you are not a great student or don't have any prior experience or connections. We will then show you the exact blueprint one of us used to land our dream job on Wall Street and how you can do the same. And, finally, you will learn how to make BIG MONEY in college while all of your peers are working for minimum wage.

First, why are internships a must?

Remember the Great Recession of 2008-2009…you know, when the economy collapsed and your parents were freaking out because their retirement accounts were cut in half? Well, even if you are not familiar with what I am talking about, just know that in 2008 our economy went into pure chaos. Companies went bankrupt and a ton of people lost their jobs. To give you a rough idea, per the Bureau of Labor Statistics, in September of 2008, over 400,000 jobs were lost. Besides being horrible for those people who were out of a job, these events have a DIRECT IMPACT ON YOU AND YOUR CAREER. All of those people who were forced out of the workforce during the recession are now getting back into it, and because their earnings have been depressed or non-existent for years, those same people are willing to work in positions for which they are overqualified. Essentially what is happening, and what will continue to happen, is entry-level jobs are receiving applicants who already have several years' experience in industry. Key point, when you get out of college and are trying to find your first job, you will be competing with people who already have much more experience than you do.

So, let's say the local software company is hiring for an entry-level position. Do you think they are going to hire a recent college graduate who has not ever stepped foot inside of a business to work, or is the company going to hire someone with several years' experience who is willing to work for the same salary of the recent grad? Of course they are going to hire the more experienced person. Like it? Don't like it? Doesn't matter, that's just how it is. In capitalism, BUSINESS DECISIONS ARE ABOUT MONEY. You may feel like this is not fair, but if you were running a company you would make the same decisions.

Basically, to put it simply: NO EXPERIENCE = NO JOB.

Ok, so that's the bad news. And now for the good news — the sooner you realize that getting experience is the name of the game, the sooner you can start getting ahead of all your peers who will ultimately be competing for the same jobs. You do this by getting your first internship, and then your second, and then your third, and then your fourth. You get the point.

What is an internship?

The first thing you have to realize about an internship is that the definition is very flexible. An internship is NOT defined by the amount of hours, or even days per week you work. Does that make sense? To be clear, you could spend 40 hours a week working in an internship, or you could spend 10 hours a week working in an internship. At the end of the day, it doesn't make a difference when it's put on your résumé … it's going to be illustrated as one internship.

There are only two important elements in an internship — (1) the applicable EXPERIENCE you acquire and (2) the DURATION (amount of days/months/years) of time you worked in the internship. All the employer cares about is whether YOU HAVE PROVEN YOURSELF at another company and that you did it for a reasonable period of time — at least three months is acceptable for an internship but six months is ideal.

This leads us to one of the most crucial parts of the internship process — developing a blueprint.

What is the internship blueprint?

Once you get into your career, you will realize there are two essential fundamentals to becoming successful — STRATEGIC PLANNING AND TACTICAL

EXECUTION. These are interdependent on one another. Lacking one equates to subpar performance in your professional and personal life. Create a strategy without tactical implementation and clearly, you will not get anything done. You could have the best plan in the world, but if there is no action to back it up, results are impossible to obtain. Conversely, if you go out and take action without any clear direction, you are likely to end up at a destination that is far off from where you initially desired. We are trying to give you the best insights into both worlds — strategic and tactical. For now, however, let's focus only on strategy.

When I was in college, I had 10 internships. I am not saying that in any way to brag or come off as superior in any way. In fact, it's quite the opposite. If I can get 10 internships, then SO CAN YOU, guaranteed! I was not gifted with a high IQ, or born into a family of money or connections. So trust me when I say you can get the same results as me, if not better, as you are most likely starting off with better resources than I had.

Long story short, I had a strategy, and so should you! The only reason I was able to get so much job experience before I graduated was purely a function of having the right strategy and then doing the legwork to fulfill the plan.

I learned this strategy when I was 18 years old, and because it changed my life, I would like to share that plan with you. But before I show you my blueprint, let's get a few things straight so you know how important this is. The strategy that I am about to tell you was given to me by a man who owned several companies on different stock exchanges. I was lucky enough to have a conversation with him, and he gave it to me straight. He told me how the world is, rather than how the world should be. Up until receiving his guidance, I was just going along being pushed through the school system, thinking that I would be taken care of. I honestly believed that my teachers and guidance counselors would hold my hand all the way to my dream job. I can tell you now, from hindsight, that thinking was flawed, and I am so happy I met this mentor and for all the insight he has shared with me that I am about to share with you.

You must understand that this strategy will give you exactly what you need to land your dream job. Be sure to pay close attention to every word and every step. You should write down this blueprint and review it often, weekly at a minimum, to ensure you don't just let it fall to the curb.

When I was 18, I thought I was on the path to Wall Street. I thought I was on the right path, and I was dead wrong. That's when I got the best advice I had ever received up to that point. My mentor, let's call him Mr. X, sat me down one day and asked the famous question — "Where do you want to be in the next five years?" Since it was a question that I had thought about very often, I spouted an answer in a fraction of a second — "Wall Street!" I said. I thought he was going to be proud that I had obviously thought through my goals and my future. Not the case. He wasn't impressed. His next question, which was his main point, was, "OK, what is your plan on getting there?" Again I quickly told him my plan, which went like this — "I'm going to be super-fantastic-awesome in my classes, graduate with a 4.0, and then get hired on Wall Street." He was even less impressed with my second answer. After he gave a little condescending chuckle, he pointed out all of the many obvious flaws I had in my so-called plan. He told me I had the right goal but I had the completely wrong blueprint.

He said "Look, just think about it logically, even if you get a 4.0, you are competing for arguably some of the top jobs in the world. There will be hundreds of thousands of students graduating at the same time you are. Many of them will come from better schools, and many of them will have relationships directly into those companies that you are telling me you want to work for. You have no shot based off of your current roadmap."

Luckily for me, he did not stop there. He continued, "Here is what I want you to do, it's pretty simple. If you want to make it to Wall Street, you will have to begin acquiring as many professional connections as you can, and you need to learn how to actually do the work that Wall Street companies value. So, if you want a shot at this, go out and get your first internship immediately, then get a new internship every six months. Don't stop, not even during your senior year."

And that was the first step of the blueprint that changed my professional life. I had no idea we were supposed to get experience, especially that volume of experience, while attending college. And let me tell you, HE WAS SPOT ON! The ONLY reason I made it to Wall Street was because of his advice. I took a ridiculously large amount of classes when I was in school. I read an astronomical amount of books in my industry since the age of 12. I got good grades. I did everything the system told me I should, and if I had stayed on that path, there would have been zero chance of me reaching my goal. All of those traditional, check-the-box milestones would have provided me little to no benefit in getting to where I wanted to go, and my guess is they will yield small results for you, so don't fall into that trap! The #1 — and I mean #1 — thing I did to launch a successful career was doing exactly what he said — GET YOUR FIRST INTERNSHIP AND GET A NEW ONE EVERY SIX MONTHS. And that is the first step of the blueprint.

Here are all of the components of the blueprint!

Step 1: Get your first internship and get a new one every six months. This will give you the depth and width of experience you need before you graduate. If you go to a four-year school, you will have eight internships and 10 if you attend a five-year program.

Step 2: Work on projects during your internships. Work on as many projects as you can during your tenure at each company. Project work is easily translated to your résumé. If you can, aim for working on three projects per internship, as this will provide you with in-depth experience and enable you to speak intelligently during your interviews for your next internship.

Step 3: Get letters of recommendation. Ideally, get a letter of recommendation after each project from the leader or manager of that project. At a minimum, request a letter of recommendation towards the end of your internship from your employer. Be sure to ask for this at least a month before your internship ends, as bosses tend to get busy and administrative tasks like this can take a while to be completed. Another tip, when requesting a letter of recommendation, INCLUDE A LETTER THAT YOU HAVE ALREADY WRITTEN so they can just sign if they want to. This may sound uncomfortable to you, but trust me, this will make the job easier for the person on the other end and nine times out of 10 they will be appreciative. If it makes it easier, word your request like this:

Dear Mr. ABC,

Thank you so much for the opportunity to work for your company. As you know, my internship will be complete at the end of this month. That said, if you feel that I have worked hard and provided value to the company, would you mind providing me with a letter of recommendation so that I may include it in my professional portfolio? I know you are unbelievably busy, so I have drafted a template for you to use if it makes it easier for you. Please feel free to use as little or as much of the template as you see fit. Thank you again for the opportunity to work here and thank you for your consideration.

Step 4: Get and keep in touch with contacts. Obtaining experience is only half the benefit of an internship. The other half is developing relationships in the professional world. Even if you are uncomfortable with "networking," it is much easier than you think.

Here is a simple plan for developing the maximum amount of relationships in your internship. SET A GOAL OF HAVING A QUALITY CONVERSATION WITH ONE NEW PERSON A WEEK. If you are really ambitious, make your goal one a day. And all I mean by a "quality conversation" is to chat with someone about more than the weather and for more than five minutes. To accomplish this, invite people out to lunch, or coffee if you are more of an introvert. You would be amazed how effective this is, even if you are not a good conversationalist! I know many of you introverts out there are damning me for this advice because I am making it seem easier than it is. Well, fellow introverts, yes, I am also in the keep-to-myself club. To make it even easier for you, here is what you do — send an email to a fellow employee that sounds like this:

> *Hey (insert employee name here),*
>
> *As part of my internship process I have a goal of meeting everyone in the company, as I am new to this industry and would like to learn as much as possible. That said, it would be great to chat with you over lunch sometime, and I would love to hear about your role within the organization. You are probably super busy, so if grabbing a coffee, or even a quick talk in the conference room, would be easier for you that works as well! Of course, if you can't fit this into your schedule, I completely understand. Hope to talk soon.*

Then, when you actually do have lunch or coffee with them, have a handful of questions ready to help guide the conversation. However, be sure not to make it too scripted. BE GENUINELY INTERESTED IN THEM and their answers. If you need more knowledge on how to develop professional relationships, I highly recommend you read the book *How to Win Friends and Influence People* by Dale Carnegie. It is a classic and will give you step-by-step instructions on how to turn yourself into a great communicator.

After you have developed the initial contact and relationship with a co-worker, stay in touch for the duration of your internship and store their contact information (LinkedIn is a great resource for doing this). Remember that most people are hired via a relationship, not a job posting.

The two pillars of finding your first internship:

Pillar 1: Develop your "core ask." The first step in finding an internship is developing what I call your *core ask*. This is just a scripted version of your request to employers for an internship. Yes, I literally mean scripted, as in premeditated and written down. This core ask will be an asset to you probably hundreds of times during your internship process. However, while a core ask is paramount, it is not complicated and should take you only 10 minutes to write up. At its foundation, it's just a concise way of asking for what you want.

The three components of a core ask are (1) stating who you are, (2) what you are looking for and (3) why they should consider your request.

Here is an example:

> Hi Mrs. ABC,
>
> My name is Joe and I am a junior at XYZ University, majoring in business (who you are). I am looking for an internship (this is the "what" part) and was wondering if you knew of any opportunities at your company this summer (why you are contacting them). If so, it would great to speak with you, as I have experience in social media marketing (or any other useful skill that they would want — this is more of the "why they should consider you" part) and I believe I could add value to your firm. If you have time to discuss this topic, I can be available at whatever day and time is convenient for you. If you are too busy, however, I completely understand and I really appreciate your consideration.

Use this framework to ask for your internships. You can use it in email and verbal form, whatever is applicable.

I understand that when you are starting out, developing your core ask can seem difficult while creating the *why they should consider hiring me* portion. Don't be nervous. The fact that you are YOUNG AND SHOWING AMBITION IS A HUGE ASSET that will overcome so many obstacles, even lack of experience. Remember that on the other side of your request is a human being. Human beings are emotional, so they are emotionally attracted to things like perseverance. If you show even the slightest bit of drive and motivation to go out of your comfort zone and do things beyond your age (like asking for an internship at the age of 18), employers will admire your ambition, regardless of your talent. Sounds corny and embellished, but it's not. It's true.

For instance, I wanted to eventually gain access to the stock exchange when I went after one of my internships, but I had absolutely no applicable experience that would be relevant to the employer. I figured my chances of actually landing the internship were close to 1%, but I figured if I didn't ask, it would be a guaranteed 0%. And, by the way, just in case you are wondering, I was unbelievably nervous to ask, so don't feel bad if you have similar feelings. Anyway, here was my core ask:

> *Hello sir, my name is Wes and I am a freshman finance major at the local university (who you are). I was wondering if you would consider hiring me as an intern (what you are looking for and why you are contacting them). I just want to be up front with you, I don't have any applicable experience in your industry, but I think I may have something that you don't ... time. Running so many companies leaves you, I imagine, with no time. I will do whatever you need, I don't care if I have to get your coffee five times a day, I will do it and you don't have to pay me anything (why they should consider you). Being immersed in the environment will be compensation enough for me. Would you be interested in hiring me as an intern?*

He hired me the next day and I was working one day later. Yes, it was literally that easy, and yes, my core ask was that elementary. The point is, don't wait. YOUR CORE ASK DOESN'T HAVE TO BE PERFECT. In fact, it shouldn't be perfect. Being perfect and too scripted will work against you, as you will sound too robotic and less like a human. Remember that your age (being young) is a huge asset to you — actually, it's probably your biggest asset — so stumbling on your words and not being completely polished will most likely work to your benefit.

REMEMBER — NOTHING BEATS HUSTLE. NOTHING.

Pillar 2: Find an internship. After developing your core ask you must then actually go out there and ask! However, you want to work smarter, not harder. There are a ton of ways to find your first gig, but they are not all equally as effective. In fact, if you use the wrong tools and resources to apply for internships, you will most likely get discouraged from lack of progress and give up before you actually yield any results. Instead of wasting a bunch of time and eventually giving up, follow this little format:

To find your first internship, consider these avenues:

1. Friends and family
2. On-campus jobs – college work study
3. Career center internship postings
4. Other websites
5. Create your own

Start with your friends and family. Finding an internship opportunity via your close personal relationships, whether it be friends or family, can be the easiest and quickest way to get into a company. You will often be able to even completely skip the interview process. You know that old saying *"It's not what you know, it's who you know"* … it's especially true when looking for an internship or a job. Before you start to create any excuses claiming you don't know anybody who could help, try writing down all the people you do know and the people they may know who could help you. Again, remember that at your age people want to help contribute to your success, so don't be afraid to ask for help. Once you have your list written down, call those contacts and just say your core ask. And voila, it could be that easy to land your first internship.

College work-study. If, for some reason, no success comes from the friends or family route, go to the next best thing — looking for jobs within your college or university. These jobs are usually called work-study positions and therefore only students at the college are eligible to apply, so your competitive pool is minimized. It is important, however, to make sure you GET A WORK-STUDY JOB THAT CAN ACTUALLY BE CONSIDERED AN INTERNSHIP.

For example, when I was in college I worked in the university's accounting department, which actually ended up being one of my best internship experiences. I had incredibly flexible hours, was able to do my homework during slow periods, and built an influential network that is still helping me today. If you are interested in pursuing this avenue, go to your college's administration offices and ask where you can learn about the work-study programs. They will show you all types of openings, most of which are going to be completely irrelevant to you, such as cafeteria assistant, gym attendant, etc. What you are interested in are the positions that will give you applicable experience in your desired industry. Just keep your eyes on the goal and always be thinking about advancing to the next step.

College career center. The next place to look is at the school's career center, where you will find an internship database from local employers. Depending on your college's relationships, you may have some great opportunities, but expect to do a lot of legwork. Without getting into the politics of the matter, most universities don't invest heavily in their career services departments, so don't be surprised if the department is understaffed. Of course, this means you will need to put in a lot of effort to land an internship even if it gets set up through the career center.

Since you might run into some roadblocks with this strategy, here is what you'll want to do:

1. Go to your career center, let them know you are interested in an internship and ask what the next steps are to proceed. If they are like most colleges, they will give you access to an internship database showing employers in the area that are interested in hiring interns from your school.

2. Once you gain access to the internship database, create a list of your top 20 opportunities. Be sure to collect all of the contact information from database.

3. Immediately email those contacts with your core ask.

4. If you don't hear back from your email by the next day, follow up with a phone call. All you have to say is:

   Hi, my name is _____, and I am calling about an internship at your company. Do you know who I would speak with regarding your internships?

Once the appropriate person is on the phone, say:

> *Hi, my name is _____. I'm sorry to bother you in the middle of the work day. I was just calling to ask about the internship opportunity at your company. Would you have time to discuss the steps I need to take to properly apply?*

Then let the conversation go where it naturally goes. You will be surprised, as you may get to interview right on the spot. It's amazing how many companies will hire interns just based off of one conversation.

Internship websites. You can certainly find internship opportunities via the internet, but realize that this strategy is not a magic bullet. It can actually be a black hole, as many internship postings on the web are often outdated, so you could often be applying to an opening that no longer exists. I'm not telling you this to discourage using these resources but just informing you so you have the appropriate expectations. You should use the internet as a supplement to your plan, not as the only vehicle.

Winning an internship on the internet is a numbers game. Decide up front the number of internships you want to apply to online, and commit to executing that number every day. I would recommend applying to 10 internships a day online. That's 50 a week. 200 a month. It's tough to lose when you are doing 200 a month of anything. But don't let this be daunting. Keep in mind that applying to any internship online usually takes just a matter of minutes. Of course there are exceptions to every rule, as some larger companies have a lengthier application process, but even still, it's just a matter of copying and pasting your résumé.

Start your own business. If you are entrepreneurial, the fastest way to get an internship is to just create your own! The funny thing is that even if you create a business that loses money, it could still be perceived as impressive experience in future interviews. Of course it must be a legitimate business in the sense that you actually executed a sound plan and had customers, but don't worry about bringing it up. AS LONG AS YOU PUT IN A TON OF EFFORT

AND CAN PROVE IT at the interview table, you've got a great story to tell, even if it includes one of failure.

At a minimum, it will help you land a future internship. This might originally sound counterintuitive to you, but keep in mind that most people at some point in their lives wished they had created a business but were too scared to do so, including those who will be interviewing you in the future. So, if anything, they will respect your hustle and ambition regardless of the net result.

Make BIG money with internships. Pay should not be an issue.

First and foremost, even if you never make any money with internships, it is 100% worth it. Getting your foot in the door, developing quality relationships, getting access to software and tools, and DEVELOPING SKILL SETS THAT YOU COULD NOT ACQUIRE INSIDE OF A CLASSROOM IS ABSOLUTELY PRICELESS. In fact, some internships offer so much value, you should actually be paying for the experience! And I am not joking even a little bit. I worked for free for about two years because I knew the future payoff would be worth it. My friends told me I was crazy. Actually, now that I think about it, even my family told me I was crazy. BUT I can say with absolute certainty, in hindsight, it was more than worth it, as it was directly because of that experience that I was able to make over $30/hour in my final internship and ultimately landed me the job on Wall Street.

Make money! If you go about getting internships in the exact way I laid out for you in the blueprint in the beginning of this chapter, it will be hard for you not to make money. And, potentially, a lot of money! So here is the three-step process to making big money in internships:

Step 1: Get experience immediately. In order for you to make money in the marketplace, you MUST SHOW THAT YOU HAVE ALREADY PROVIDED VALUE IN THE MARKETPLACE. You do this by getting your first internship. If you can get paid for this first internship, great. If you can't get paid for this first internship, great. All that matters is getting the initial experience. If you are unsure of how to obtain your first internship, see the <u>how to find your first internship section</u> in this chapter.

Step 2: Acquire as many USEFUL skills as possible. This is how you become valuable to companies. It's pretty simple. If a company has a need, and you are able to fill that need, you will get paid. Your compensation will be commensurate with the amount of value you provide to the organization. For example, if the only value you provide is the ability to get coffee or take out the trash, you will be paid around minimum wage, if you are paid anything. Why? Because the marketplace does not see those activities as very valuable. Like it? Not like it? Doesn't matter … that's just the way it is. Similarly, if you are providing a solution for a highly valued need, you will be paid accordingly. For example, if you are a programmer, a pretty technical skill set that few people possess, you will be paid a higher amount.

Of course, the next logical question is **how do you acquire valuable skill sets that companies will pay you handsomely for?** I know of three definite ways of accomplishing this:

First, get a college education. Given that most, if not all, of you reading this book are most likely in college, recently finished or planning on going to college, I am preaching to the choir here, so no need to expand on this. Go to college — period. Don't be one of those ridiculous people who say that college isn't worth it. These people are just using anecdotal evidence that focuses on the anomalies (the Mark Zuckerbergs of the world) rather than rationally looking at the masses of individuals who have drastically increased their earnings potential specifically because they got a college education.

Second, always be working in the real world. In your case, this means committing to getting an internship and always having one during your entire college career. You must understand that while a college education is paramount, it is not sufficient. You MUST be in the real world working on real-time problems. The sooner you realize academia is a laggard to the marketplace, and always will be, the sooner you will start making money. Employers are more likely to pay you and PAY YOU AN INCREASED AMOUNT

IF THEY ARE CONVINCED YOU HAVE A HIGHLY VALUED SKILL SET, and the way you convince them is by showing that you have already worked for other companies.

If you really want to make a lot of money during your internships, become an expert in an area that is highly valued to a company and that not many students (aka your competitors) are yet skilled in. I will give you a hint — this opportunity usually exists around technology. Since technology is obviously the foundation of most companies today, there is a huge need for people who know how to use it.

The problem for companies, and the opportunity for you, is the biggest generation currently working in those companies is not great at using technology. Your generation was basically born with a cell phone in their hands, so you already have a better fundamental knowledge of technology than most working professionals. Trust me, you would be amazed at the number of employees who still have trouble using Microsoft Word. It's actually kind of troubling, but nonetheless, it's great news for you!

To take advantage of this technological generational disparity, find out what technology is highly valued in the specific industry you are in, and become an expert in it. For example, if you are a finance major, learn how to use a Bloomberg terminal (software used at pretty much every trading desk in the U.S.) so you will be of the 1% of college students who know how to use that crucial tool in the financial world. Think this will increase your worth to a company? Absolutely.

Step 3: Get certifications desired in your industry. I will expose to you a dirty little secret that colleges really don't want you to realize — there are well over a million students graduating every year from college. By definition, this means that AN UNDERGRADUATE COLLEGE DEGREE IS A COMMODITY. In other words, you must find a way to differentiate yourself academically from your peer group. Besides the ways we already mentioned in this chapter, the final significant way to acquire a valuable, highly paid skill set is to OBTAIN INDUSTRY CERTIFICATIONS.

There are certifications and professional designations in every field that instantly increase your attractiveness to companies. The Charter Financial Analyst (CFA) designation in finance is an example of this. Whatever the industry is, I assure you, it will have its hierarchy of certifications. My advice to you would be to focus on the top designations, which are usually the most difficult to obtain, as they will be the most valued in your industry. Some certifications, like the CFA, have certain age requirements and professional criteria required before you can obtain the designation, so make sure you know all of the prerequisites ahead of time.

Finally, if you have done these three steps, there is only one thing left to do. ASK FOR BIG MONEY! I know this sounds elementary, but oftentimes all you have to do to make more money in an internship is ask for it! If you have highly valued and needed skills, then you can and should be compensated accordingly, regardless of your age or current level in college. I can tell you right now a ton of underpaid people exist in the world solely due to the fact they have not asked for higher compensation.

I know asking for a raise or a higher starting salary is an uncomfortable situation, but most of that is due to lack of preparation. If you want to make this easier on yourself, before you ask for higher pay, write down the top 10 reasons why you deserve that pay, in order of importance (highest to lowest), and tell those reasons to your employer.

Whatever method you choose for requesting more money, do it. If you know you have followed all of the advice above — you've got the academic background, a highly valued skill set, and the proven experience with certifications to back it up, there is only one thing left to do. Ask for it.

Chapter 3: Secret #3

Hard Work — It Pay$ Off

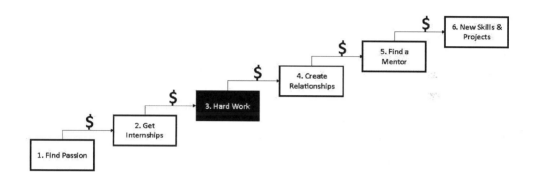

Hard work beats talent when talent doesn't work hard.

—Tim Notke
High school basketball coach

What would you do if you failed at something 10 times? Would you continue to work hard until you were successful? How about 25 times? 50 times? Would you keep going? Or would you give up? The answer will probably depend on how much passion you have for what you do. Very few people or companies become successful overnight. It can take a while and usually involves many trials and errors. That is the case with Finnish startup company Rovio. You might recognize the company name because they are responsible for creating one of the most successful gaming apps in history — *Angry Birds.*

Angry Birds has been downloaded OVER 2 BILLION TIMES and brings in BILLIONS OF DOLLARS OF REVENUE from merchandise, movies and cartoons. What most people don't know is that this company spent six years trying to produce a successful game. THEY FAILED 51 TIMES before hitting the jackpot! *Angry Birds* was their 52nd attempt and the game quickly became a global phenomenon. The company started as a mobile gaming company and eventually became a media entertainment company due to the success of the game.

But what if the developers and employees had given up and decided to call it quits after one of their 51 unsuccessful attempts? What if they stopped working hard to create something great? Then you AND 2 BILLION OTHER PEOPLE wouldn't have *Angry Birds to enjoy* to burn time during that General Philosophy 101 course or that avoidable "all hands" meeting. And the company? Well, it wouldn't be the success it is or even in existence today, and all of its employees would be now working somewhere else. Just remember that the next time you sling Chuck, the yellow speed bird, into a bunch of bricks and wood in Level 2.

We know, "hard work" sounds cliché and probably is advice you have received before. It certainly isn't anything new or ground breaking, but it's essential. You will read first-hand accounts about how hard work paid off for all those we have interviewed, launching them on careers to making over $100K.

I received my first promotion only after I was recognized for the hard work I had performed the prior 12 months for both my company and client. I had worn multiple hats, serving in a variety of roles for my client, pretty much anything that was asked. I was pushed to my limit by my direct report — a historically challenging client to please who was about 40 years older and more experienced than me. He was extremely intelligent, highly respected but also demanding and had high expectations for everyone.

Sitting on just the other side of the cubicle wall next to him, I was always on the edge of my seat, every day working hard to win him over with my work. I had to know my stuff and carefully communicate things the correct way. Details were extremely important to him and my job. And guess what? IT COULDN'T HAVE STARTED OFF ANY WORSE! I didn't think I was going to make it past the first week or be able to rebound from a mistake I made and how pissed off I made him. But I gradually won him over with my hard work, and as time went on he was able to visibly see and hear about that hard work from those in the office and others we did business with. Where others had been unsuccessful, I was able to excel.

Looking back on it, this is where I learned the true definition of hard work. He soon became a good friend, mentor and advocate to my team and me. He was on our side. With him having such a strong influence around the office on key decisions, I am convinced had the work not been put into creating this key company-client relationship (yes, hard work can involve the creation of key relationships), I would not have received a promotion, a $9,000 raise and $2,000 bonus at year end. More importantly, I would not have the work ethic I do today, had I not gone through this experience.

Allow us to make a key distinction. While it's OK to stop doing work that you are not passionate about, it's NOT OKAY to run from hard work if it is part of your passion. If I ran after week 1, I can tell you I wouldn't be here — probably not writing this book and sharing this story with you.

Here's the thing about hard work: If you don't work hard, then you probably don't love what you do. This is a recipe for becoming stagnant and complacent with your job and that will lead to zero or modest raises. Is that where you want to be? Is that where you want to go? If you do work hard, then the OPPORTUNITIES WILL FOLLOW. Opportunities to grow, to be promoted and to make more money. Those opportunities may not necessarily be right in front of you at your current place of employment. Which is why THE BEST TIME TO LOOK FOR A JOB IS WHEN YOU ALREADY HAVE ONE, while you are performing hard work with measurable results that you can communicate during interviews.

I have studied thousands of career tracks both in my own networks and through the market research I conduct. I estimate that nearly 75% of those individuals changed companies for a promotional movement. Why do people change companies? Either they hate their current job or they found a better opportunity with a new employer who will better reward them for their past performance — their hard work. With the amount of money that companies and organizations spend on recruiting, interviewing and training efforts, I've always been amazed that they allow some of their best and most talented employees to walk away. It should never get to this point. But it happens — all the time. Loyalty of companies to employees and employees to companies is extremely rare in the 21st century. Practically gone are the days of staying with the same company for 40-plus years as my father, Jim Quinlan, did with GlaxoSmithKline.

Another way to look at hard work is performing more service than what one is paid. How many times have you heard someone say, "That's not in my job description" or "They are not paying me to do that so screw it" or "That's below or above my pay grade"? I know I'm guilty of having these thoughts, preventing me from being a more productive employee in the past. If you follow this approach of providing more value than the amount you are paid, it will be visible to employers and they will compete for your services.

Let this sink in for a minute. THERE WILL BE COMPETITION FOR YOU. If there is competition amongst multiple employers for your services, then you ultimately have bargaining power. Bargaining power used in negotiating can help increase your earnings by going back and forth between two offers, playing them against each other and ultimately choosing the best one. I've seen this happen with several contacts across different industries. They performed more work and provided more value to the company for which they were being paid. They then took that experience, skill set and value and either turned it into a promotion or brought it to a new company that offered more money for their services.

HARD WORK, OVER TIME, ALWAYS PAYS OFF. ALWAYS. Read that sentence over again and notice the two essential components: HARD WORK and OVER TIME. Hard work must be done consistently over an extended period of time in order to see results. This DOES NOT ALWAYS MEAN working the longest amount of hours (sometimes it does) but rather BEING THE MOST PRODUCTIVE VERSION OF YOURSELF IN THE HOURS WHICH YOU WORK. It is said that it takes years to become an overnight success, and that is completely true. We tend to think that people who become successful just hit one big break in a short period of time, when in reality, they have worked for years with little-to-no results and then finally started gaining momentum bit by bit. In a world filled with shortcuts, magical weight loss pills and silver bullet solutions, you know hard work sounds painful, and you are absolutely right. HARD WORK IS PAINFUL. HARD WORK IS UNCOMFORTABLE, AND YES, HARD WORK IS INCONVENIENT.

When your friends want to go out all the time and party, you will have to work on certain occasions. You will have to work nights and weekends at times. You will have to experience failure and learn how to start over. Yes, hard work is all of these things that don't feel good, which is exactly why hard work is so rare, but that's also why extraordinary results are so rare.

The bad news is anything worthwhile requires a TON of hard work. The great news is because so much effort is required, not many people want to put in the time nor the work, so the opportunity is open to literally anyone willing to take it. BE ONE OF THOSE PEOPLE. Commit, right now, to not being one of those people who accepts mediocrity. Commit to something greater. Commit to creating something larger than yourself. COMMIT TO HARD WORK!

Chapter 4: Secret #4 Creating & Fo$tering Relation$hip$

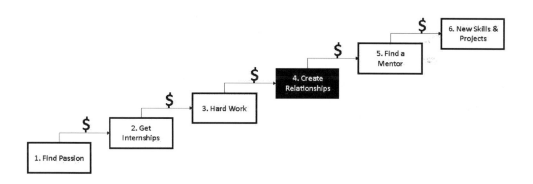

The way we communicate with others and with ourselves ultimately determines the quality of our lives.

—Anthony Robbins
Motivational speaker, personal finance instructor and self-help author

Creating and fostering relationships is an essential skill. Actually, let's rephrase that — it is THE ESSENTIAL SKILL. Go talk to anyone who is successful, no matter the industry, and they will tell you their success came from the help of another person or people. Someone helped them get the interview, connected them to the CEO of XYZ company, and mentored them along the way ... whatever the circumstance, ANOTHER HUMAN BEING GOT THEM TO WHERE THEY ARE TODAY. The sooner you realize you can't reach the top without standing on the shoulders of others, the sooner you will be on the road to greatness.

Look at all the great superstars of our time, Tom Brady, Ronda Rousey, Larry Page, Oprah Winfrey, Elon Musk, Steve Jobs — all of them, without exception, had mentors, coaches and connections to launch them into dominating their respective fields. Don't be foolish and think you can do this on your own. That's just your ego talking. And I am not pointing fingers.

For the first several years of my career I thought I could fight my way to the top. I had a competitive, rather than a collaborative, mindset. While I got a few career "wins" under my belt with this philosophy, my drive to succeed led me into a brick wall I couldn't get over alone. After realizing I needed support, I asked peers in the office, and I heard crickets ... nobody wanted to help. At the time, I couldn't believe it. How in the world could I have done all of the work for years, coming in early and leaving late, executing all of my major projects to perfection and ahead of schedule, volunteering for work that wasn't even my responsibility, taking on work that was above my pay grade, and still not get to the next level?

"How could this happen?" I thought to myself. Turns out, in my crazed obsession with getting ahead, I stepped on many people in the process. I wasn't malicious to anybody, but I certainly wasn't friendly and supportive either. My short-sighted strategy left me defeated without anyone to turn to.

Having the me-against-the-world mentality may sound good to a competitive person, but it produces ZERO RESULTS in the long run, and I learned that lesson the hard way.

On the other side of the equation, I have also experienced what it's like to have harmonious, quality relationships with people. There is no comparison, this is where you want to be. Not only does it feel better to work WITH people, rather than AGAINST people, it produces MASSIVE RESULTS. In fact, I will let you in on a secret that few people know about me. I got to Wall Street NOT because of an excellent résumé, or because of a great track record in the finance industry or due to the school I attended. No, none of those reasons. The MAIN REASON I landed a job on Wall Street was because a friend of mine put a phone call into her friend at the company. IF IT WASN'T FOR THAT RELATIONSHIP I WOULD HAVE NEVER WORKED ON WALL STREET. To put it simply, because of that single relationship, my career took off.

When you hear the term *networking* thrown around in college or the workplace, how does it make you feel? It almost has a negative connotation to it, because so often people make it feel forced when in reality, it should feel natural, when done the right way. To the masses, networking means attending a social function such as an office party with the goal of meeting as many people as possible in a short amount of time. To others, it means going to lunch with a co-worker who is already your friend and talking about lame Hollywood gossip and relationships (see the Kardashians and John Mayer) or why the running back on your fantasy football team decided to take a knee on the 1 yard line instead of going for the touchdown. Didn't the player know that you had him in your starting lineup with the championship on the line? Of course he didn't because it wasn't important and neither is that conversation for your career.

There is a time and a place for those conversations, but to spend valuable time on them when you have the opportunity to create a much more valuable relationship that will benefit you is ill-advised. While showing up and seeing who embarrasses themselves the most at the company party after downing too many white wine spritzers is entertaining and makes for a great story, it will NOT provide you with the meaningful relationships needed to get on the fast track to launching your career.

Whereas many people shoot for a large "quantity" of relationships, I would urge you to FOCUS ON THE "QUALITY" OF THE RELATIONSHIPS INSTEAD. Of course, developing deep relationships with the RIGHT PEOPLE, as opposed to shallow relationships with many people, is easier said than done. It takes time and effort (and hard work) to create a meaningful connection with someone — which is exactly why many people don't do it. While it is challenging, it is certainly not impossible, and there is a method you can follow, which is listed in great detail in Dale Carnegie's *How to Win Friends and Influence People*. However, here are some key takeaways from that book you can start using now:

1. LEARN PEOPLE'S NAMES, write them down, and address them by their name the next time you see them. If it helps, try spelling their name or ask for a business card.
2. Actually LISTEN TO PEOPLE WHEN THEY TALK, don't just wait for them to stop talking so you can start talking. Your cell phone belongs in your pocket or purse in these conversations.
3. When someone does something well, SHOUT ABOUT IT! Make it known to them and everyone else who can hear you. People like to feel appreciated. Celebrate their success. It gives them a feeling of importance.
4. Be real with people. Nobody likes people who act fake, and you can instantly spot people who are phony. Don't let this be you. Do whatever you can to FIND THINGS ABOUT A PERSON THAT MAKE YOU AUTHENTICALLY INTERESTED IN THEM.

These all sound like simple points, but DO NOT UNDERESTIMATE THEIR POWER. Go and test it for yourself and you see exactly what we are talking about. Those are just a few of the main lessons in the book, but they will get you started.

Another good habit is to ALWAYS BE COLLECTING DOTS (ABCD) — dots of information on people you meet. Keep notes on people. It may sound odd at first but it's how the entire online retail industry thrives through the tactic called remarketing where companies get you to buy their stuff through customized advertisements and emails based on your viewing and purchase history. In other words, your Amazon.com account is not just randomly suggesting you buy a new pair of Nike running sneakers, it's because you bought workout clothes last month and the company knows that you, like most people will tend to buy these items together. Don't remember making this purchase? That's because those grey shoes with the neon swoosh are still sitting in your online shopping cart. You didn't really think the company had some type of psychic power, did you? Of course not — all of these dots of information are stored in a customer relationship management (CRM) system.

Here is how YOU CAN USE THIS STRATEGY IN YOUR OWN LIFE. Similar to a hotel or upscale restaurant, you should keep your own personal CRM system and fill it with specific information about all of your key contacts. For example, let's say you go out to lunch with an executive at your company. AS SOON AS THE MEETING IS OVER, before you go to your car, check your text messages or even use the bathroom, you should WRITE DOWN EVERYTHING YOU CAN REMEMBER about the person — or even easier, speak the info into a note-taking app (Evernote works great for this), and save it. How long does that take? Maybe about 30-60 seconds.

How long does it take to forget most of the things discussed after your meeting is over and you get back to your routine called life? About 30-60 seconds. So what will you choose — will you remember to do this or will you forget, essentially making most of meeting and time investment meaningless?

FOLLOW UP. You should have a follow up system with a reminder to check in with each person you meet every so often. You determine the appropriate frequency. Here's a golden nugget for you — sending a copy of a book you have read and enjoyed relative to the conversation you had is a great idea to stand out from the crowd. Why? Because VERY FEW PEOPLE DO THIS!

Going a step further, place a note in the specific pages you want them to read. He or she will be impressed and appreciative. You will be perceived highly of because you're connecting the conversation you had to a book to further benefit the person. You're giving them value and the gesture says, "I care." That is showing a GENUINE INTEREST in them. It likely will come back to you someday, as they will not forget this when you need something in return.

AND PAY! If you requested or suggested the meeting over coffee or a meal to meet or learn something from somebody else, YOU SHOULD ALWAYS PAY! You know that moment that sometimes can get awkward? When the waiter places the bill on the center of the table and you look at each other, then look away, hesitate for 7 seconds, then decide to split the bill, or even worse, have the other person PayPal or Venmo you $9.95 because they got an espresso AND an extra side of bacon with their Western omelet? Shit, did they really need to eat two sources of pig? Well it's only awkward because you let it be awkward.

Don't be cheap. PEOPLE DON'T LIKE CHEAP PEOPLE. I find it amazing that many people are willing to pay $7-$12 for a beer or cocktail at a restaurant, concert or sporting event yet are reluctant to own a similar bill when they asked someone to meet for lunch. While it is usually a long-term strategy, covering the bills can lead to opportunities. START THINKING WITH THE LONG TERM IN MIND.

So why is this important? Because most people don't do it — that is why! If most people don't do something and you do, YOU WILL STAND OUT from others and people WILL LIKE YOU. Standing out is what it's all about (and no I didn't purposely just try to bust-a-rhyme). By being at the top of somebody else's mind, your relationships will be stronger for it. You only have strong relationships with people who like you. If people like you, they will go to bat for you when you ask for advice or need a favor such as a referral for a great job opportunity. Why is it important that people like you? Because in the competitive world we live in today, having someone on your side can be the deciding factor in getting accepted into that MBA program, getting that promotion with the 10% pay increase or landing that awesome job that can be a game-changer for your career.

IT ALWAYS COMES DOWN TO WHO YOU KNOW — and this is especially true when it comes to job opportunities. Every single person — without exception — I have referred to my previous employer was hired pretty much immediately. Without my recommendation, these people would have had to go through many rounds of time-consuming interviews and may have never landed the job. The reason for them getting hired is simple — my company liked me and trusted that someone I referred to them would have a similar work ethic and values that aligned with the company. Trust was in place to make this an easier decision for them. The company saved time and money on recruiting, my buddies got jobs, and I enhanced my value to those relationships. It was a win, win, win situation. These scenarios happen all the time, and you want to be at the center of them.

The beautiful thing about creating relationships is you don't have to already know somebody. While it is certainly preferable, you can build connections with people you don't even know yet, and then foster those relationships over time.

Here's how. Let's say your dream job is to become a software engineer for Google or Microsoft. What's to stop you from doing a quick search on LinkedIn to see who living in your area holds that exact job? Send them a personal message. It may seem uncomfortable at first but as we have all heard before — GOOD THINGS HAPPEN WHEN WE TAKE OURSELVES OUTSIDE THE WALLS OF OUR COMFORT ZONE. Introduce yourself, ask for a half hour of their time by taking them out for coffee or breakfast. When you meet with them, listen to their story of how they arrived at where they are now. Thank them for their time and PAY THE BILL. Lastly, follow up with them to keep the relationship going. In the future, when the time is right, ask if they know of any internship or job opportunities and if they would consider referring you.

A résumé walked down the hall by a current employee and placed on a desk of a recruiter stands a much better chance of scoring an interview (and getting the job) than applying online where most résumés go into a black hole and never get a response or do get one but it's an automated email alerting you to the fact that you're not under consideration for the job. I don't know about you, but I don't like either of those outcomes after spending hours on job applications and résumés.

I've been on the other end of this as well. A few years ago, I applied to what at the time was my dream job to be a business teacher at a large high school in Pennsylvania. I was excited because I had so much going for me in the recruiting process: I was referred by a friend, had previously met the department head and had more applicable experience than my competitors. My interviews went as well as they possibly could. I thought I was a lock for the job. I even went out and bought 25 individual tubs of Play-Doh I had planned to use as an ice-breaker activity for the first class. I waited for them to call back. However, the school had different plans. After a week of waiting, I received that dreaded email:

Dear Candidate,

Thank you for your interest in the business teacher opportunity at _____ high school. I regret to inform you that you are no longer being considered for the position of business teacher. Please continue to monitor and apply for additional opportunities within the _____ school district.

(Electronically signed) Decision Maker, who did not write this email

Wow! I went from "a lock" to "in shock" in half a second after I read the words "Dear Candidate." IT WAS PAINFUL. So what the hell happened here, and what was I going to do with all of that damn Play-Doh? Turns out my main competitor, who got the job, had a family member working at the high school — actually, multiple family members. And in this particular district, relationships are essential to getting hired. Case in point — BUILD THE STRONGEST RELATIONSHIPS YOU CAN WITH THE RIGHT PEOPLE. Relationships are everything. Sometimes they are the only thing. The un-opened Playdoh in my room serves as a constant reminder for me to continue to create and maintain strong relationships. Someday I will open it.

Chapter 5: Secret #5
Get Your$elf a Mentor

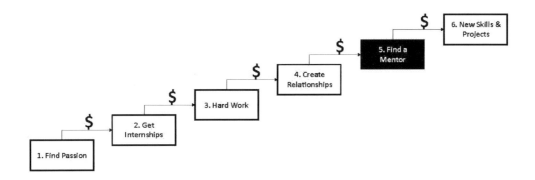

One of the greatest values of mentors is the ability to see ahead what others cannot see and to help them navigate a course to their destination.

—John C. Maxwell
New York Times best-selling author, speaker & pastor

In the previous chapter, we covered the importance of developing quality relationships. It's pretty amazing what you can learn from having a conversation with other people. However, time is scarce and we can't possibly meet with everybody when jobs and schedules get in the way. Choosing those people wisely will determine what and how much you will actually learn. And that's where the principle of having a mentor comes in. You can have one mentor or you can have several. I have mentors for different subject areas where they are needed. For example, I have a mentor for health and fitness, relationships, family situations, finance and a mentor for career advice.

Everybody needs a mentor. Let me rephrase that ... EVERYBODY WHO WANTS TO BE SUCCESSFUL NEEDS A MENTOR. If Michael Jordan, Warren Buffett, Bill Gates and countless other super-successful people all have coaches and mentors, then so should you and me. Navigating your career can be challenging and tedious at times, but the journey can be much easier with the guided hand of a mentor. The advice from someone who has been there before, done what you are trying to do, overcame the failures you will inevitably encounter and ultimately reached the success you are striving for is PRICELESS. They have already played the game and therefore already know how to win. The amount of money and time this person can save you is so great that it's hard to measure.

Just a few minutes of conversation with a seasoned pro in your field can literally save you years because they help fill what is called your *mental blind spot*.

Let me explain.... Years ago there was a study done by Harvard University showing your circle of knowledge. The circle was segmented into three parts:

"You know what you know," "You know what you don't know," and *"You don't know what you don't know."*

That sounds like a bunch of gibberish, so see the descriptions below:

"Know What You Know" (KK) — This is pretty self-explanatory. This body of information fits inside of your actual knowledge. For example, in the world of math, you may know algebra. You have studied algebra, practiced algebra and could teach algebra. *You know algebra.*

"Know What You Don't Know" (KDK) — Here it gets a little trickier. This body of information sits outside of your actual knowledge but you at least *know it exists*. Staying consistent with the math theme, you may know geometry exists, but you have no idea how to actually do any exercises in geometry. You don't know geometry but you know that you don't know geometry. To rephrase it, *you know that you don't know geometry.*

"You Don't Know What You Don't Know" (DKDK) — This is that area that is called your *mental blind spot.* This body of information comprises things you don't even know exist and wouldn't otherwise know without reading, studying or speaking to somebody else who has more knowledge in this area. For example, as stated above, you may know algebra, you may know that geometry exits but don't have a working knowledge it, and you have no idea that calculus exists until someone tells you about it. Calculus, in this example, would be representative of an area that you don't know, and *you don't know that you don't know it*.

It is the last area, the DKDK area, that is the biggest threat to our success, and it represents more than half of our total knowledge. This means that we have no clue about the majority of information out there!

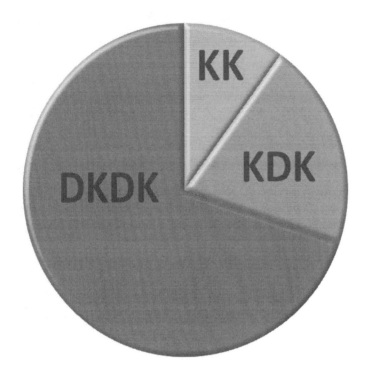

This is exactly where the VALUE OF HAVING A MENTOR COMES INTO PLAY — THEY HELP FILL IN YOUR MENTAL BLIND SPOT! A great mentor will listen to your goals and help you get there by filling in your knowledge gaps along the way. For instance, you may currently have a goal of making $100,000 a year but have no idea what careers will actually pay you that kind of money. That's what this book is for, to bring you mentors who have already reached this goal, and they are going to share with you the exact paths they took. To put it differently, they are helping you fill in some of your mental blind spot. After completing this book, you will have learned strategies, short-cuts and secrets that will expedite your path to success. A great mentor will do the same thing.

So how do you go about finding a career mentor?

Take a similar approach used to finding your first internship discussed in Chapter 2. Ideally, you will want to find a mentor who is knowledgeable and experienced in your career field or a related career field. This way, they can offer advice and insight to your challenges, opportunities and serve as a sounding board for scenarios that will be sure to come up over the course of your career. Remember, they have already been there, done that and seen most of it all.

For example, let's pretend you're a senior in college studying mechanical engineering. You've already found your passion and know that you want to pursue engineering. You already had your first internship and are currently in process of completing your second. You work hard and have put in an effort to create strong relationships with those around you. To summarize, you're serious about your career and this would be clear to anyone you have a conversation with. Since you have made this a priority, YOU'RE ALREADY MORE THAN HALF-WAY THERE TO FINDING YOUR MENTOR, YOU JUST DON'T KNOW IT YET. Next, make a list of all the people you know and place them into categories listed below. Now, let's take a closer look at those categories:

1. Family members and relatives
2. Teachers, professors and coaches
3. A friend's family members and relatives
4. Co-worker at a company you work or intern for

Family members and relatives. Start with those closest to you – it's often the easiest and fastest mentor-mentee relationship you can develop. You can still have other mentors outside of your inner circle but identifying your first mentor sooner than later is the name of the game here. Do you have a parent, grandparent, uncle, aunt or older brother or sister who knows or understands your career field? If so, great! You just found your first career mentor. If no one in your family fits the bill, then continue thinking of other people under the next category.

Teachers, professors and coaches. Remember the great teacher, professor or coach you really enjoyed or admired? Well, chances are you did well in their class or on the field or court for them too. Most teachers, professors and coaches are highly knowledgeable in their fields and often have a ton of experience they can share with you. Consider their profession: they are educators. Most people become educators to help the learning and development process of others whom they are teaching. For these reasons, they make for great mentor candidates. You may have to let these relationships grow organically over time. To put it differently, it won't become a mentor-mentee relationship as quickly as calling up a family member. A good starting place is sitting down with them during office hours to discuss career paths and learn about them and their background. Keep in mind many students don't take advantage of office hours, yet professors have to keep them and all teachers have a prep period. This will be your best opportunity to get in the door and build something that will help you in the long run. If you burned bridges with teachers by playing pranks on them and none of your professors know who you are because you stayed up all night drinking countless cans of Mountain Dew while playing World of Warcraft and sleeping through their class, then let's focus on growing up as we move onto the next category.

A friend's family members and relatives. For this one you will need the help of a friend. Once you know the career field you are passionate about pursuing, ask your friends if they have any family members or relatives in the same or similar field. If they can connect you with someone they know, you're in business. It will be helpful if they can make an introduction whether in person or by email. However, DON'T SPEND TOO MUCH TIME WAITING FOR THE INTRODUCTION TO HAPPEN. GET THE PERSON'S CONTACT INFORMATION AND SEND THEM AN EMAIL YOURSELF. Be brief and to the point. Introduce yourself. Tell them you are a friend of whatever your friend's name is and give a brief description of you and what you're studying or where you're working. Finally, ask them if they would have availability to meet for coffee to learn more about their career and answer a few questions.

Co-workers. When you start working or interning at companies, you will see there are many different types of people in the office. Some will possess poor habits and destructive attitudes that will make you wonder how any recruiter or hiring manager in their right mind gave them a job. Then there will be others who demonstrate great habits and positive attitudes. These are the people want to meet and learn from. Here's the great thing about the outlook of these people as a potential mentor – THEY ARE ALREADY IN YOUR FIELD AND EXPERIENCED. You're already in the same door, at the same building at similar times during the day. Now it's what you make of the opportunity and applying what you learned in Chapter 4. Also, if this person is your boss, it is recommended to do everything possible to make him or her look good. If you are effective in doing so, he or she will be more inclined to give you advice to make you even more productive and successful in your career.

Why will any of these people want to help mentor you?

Because if you take the approach detailed in this chapter, PEOPLE WILL BE MORE INCLINED TO HELP YOU IF THEY KNOW THIS MATTERS TO YOU AND LISTEN TO WHAT THEY HAVE TO SAY – that it won't be a waste of their time. They will not be getting paid to be your mentor but the reward for them will be to see you progress on your career journey to becoming a success – one which they can take pride in as well.

How frequently should you be in contact with your mentor?

A good rule of thumb is at least 1-2 times per month. Use common sense here – realize that your mentor has other commitments and can't possibly speak to you every day but don't let the relationship grow stale at the same time. However, as you become more experienced, the need to meet with your mentor at that level of frequency may decrease. You may find yourself checking in by shooting them a quick email or giving them a call every couple of months. At other times, like when weighing multiple job opportunities, the frequency may increase and he or she will be understanding of that scenario. Try to meet with them in person at least once a year. There is something to be said for meeting with someone in person. If you need to, DRIVE OR FLY TO THEM – IT WILL BE WORTH YOUR INVESTMENT. As a last resort, if it is not geographically or financially possible to meet in person, connect with them over Skype, Google Hangout or some other type of video call. Don't rely on email as a means for communication as it will be more time consuming for the person to write back to you than to have a conversation. Plus the interpersonal connection will make the relationship much stronger and increase the likelihood of it continuing in the future.

Lastly, if not already obvious – BE GENUINELY INTERESTED IN THEM AND GET TO KNOW THEM! Ask them about their stories, careers and challenges. Many people enjoy talking about themselves and you can only learn from them by listening.

Can you operate without a mentor? Sure you can, but even as the great Isaac Newton once said,

> *If I have seen further than others, it is by standing upon the shoulders of giants.*

Simply put, why make things more difficult for yourself than they need to be? Stand on the shoulders of your giant — the shoulders of your mentor.

Chapter 6: Secret #6

Learning New $kills & Taking on Project$

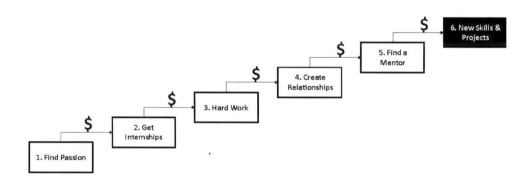

The quickest way to become an old dog is to stop learning new tricks.

—John Rooney

Just in case you are confused about this, KNOWLEDGE and SKILLS are two very different things, and they are BOTH PARAMOUNT TO YOUR SUCCESS. Knowledge in a particular field (finance, engineering, marketing, etc.) gives you the ability to understand the content and intricacies of a given field. For example, if you work in finance you want to have knowledge of interest rates, stocks, bonds, etc. However, that knowledge alone won't do you much good if you don't have the SKILLS, such as creating spreadsheets, conducting research and presenting, to put that knowledge to work.

While this sounds like an elementary topic, it is perhaps the biggest barrier to career advancement. Most people in the workplace assume that graduating from college is their ticket to a wonderful career on a constant upward trend of pay raises and promotions. THOSE PEOPLE ARE WRONG. Yes, exceptions aside, graduating from college is the prerequisite for you to get your foot into the door, but don't be confused, a degree is necessary but it is certainly not sufficient for long-term progression.

The fact that you have gone to college confirms to an employer that you have a baseline KNOWLEDGE but absolutely does not confirm you have any SKILLS THAT ARE VALUABLE TO THE COMPANY. Basically, proof of knowledge gets you in the door, consistent proof of skills keep you in the door AND GETS YOU PROMOTED!

So if skills are so important, which ones should you acquire? Should you go and increase your skill at public speaking? How about learning to code software? Maybe getting better at project management? Unfortunately there is not enough time in the day to acquire all skills in the universe. Fortunately, though, there is a shortcut. It's not about acquiring all skills. IT'S ABOUT ACQUIRING THE SKILLS MOST VALUED AT YOUR COMPANY OR INDUSTRY. How do you find out what those skills are? It's pretty simple: go to your boss, mentor or even a quick Google search, and ask the question, "What are the top three most valuable skills in this job?" I know it sounds super simple, which it is, but it also happens to be super effective.

Once you know the top skills needed in your occupation, it is time to go and actually acquire those skills. Sign up for a skills-based class (programming, for example) or management skills training where you will learn problem solving and prioritization techniques, or volunteer for a project. Do whatever creative action is necessary for you to start building skills in those areas. Dedicate a certain amount of time per week, at least 7 hours a week (just 1 hour a day) when you will work on building a specific skill within your profession. It's amazing how simple it is, but so few people actually do it. FYI, if you are thinking, "I just don't have the time to dedicate an hour a day...." or anything similar to that, just stop where you are at. There is no room for excuses.

When I began my first job in Corporate America in the management consulting industry, I started out performing and supporting internal business development work, which involved intensive technical writing in the form of proposals for the company to acquire new work. After two months, I was presented with my first client-billable project opportunity by my performance manager. It was known around the department as the "Sudan Project." For anyone who doesn't know how the consulting industry works, being billable (the number of hours charged to a client divided by the number of hours in a given time period) is a key metric to staying in the good graces of the human resources and leadership teams. This is also known as your "utilization rate." If one doesn't maintain an 80%-90% utilization rate for the year without a compelling reason, then you likely don't stick around too long. It is part of the game and how the firm makes money, increasing the bottom line.

The Sudan project was growing both in size and scope and needed an additional junior-level analyst to support project responsibilities. By the management above me, it had been portrayed to me as a "good learning opportunity" — which it was. To my peers at the office who were more transparent, this project had its fair share of issues and had been through a revolving cycle of analysts, three in the previous 12 months. I would be the fourth. Translation — no analyst or consultant wanted to work on this project!

After hearing this, I wasn't the most confident that I wanted to either. But after speaking to my dad (one of my mentors) and gaining a boost of confidence and support, I decided to accept the project opportunity. While it was true that the project lacked strong leadership and was excessively micromanaged, I LEARNED MANY NEW TRANSFERABLE SKILLS. Some of those included project communications, accounting analysis, contract procurement, scheduling, international business operations, payroll support and relationship building. I gained critical experience using Microsoft Office tools such as Access, Excel, PowerPoint, Project and managing online security portals. I stuck with the project for 14 months. I worked my ass off, often performing the work of the project manager who was being paid handsomely above me (remember — provide more service for which you are being paid). You will read later on in Chapter 7 during the interview with Lou Redwood just HOW IMPORTANT WORKING A LEVEL ABOVE YOUR JOB CAN BE WHEN TRYING TO GET ON THE FAST TRACK OF ADVANCING YOUR CAREER.

Then, an incredible thing happened. After realizing that continuing to work on that project would be impossible for me to grow, I BEGAN SEARCHING FOR NEW PROJECTS. I was eventually presented with a new opportunity to move onto another billable project with the U.S. Department of State. As I mentioned earlier, TAKING ON NEW PROJECTS OFTEN LEADS TO THE ACQUISITION OF NEW SKILLS. Adding these new skills will increase your value to prospective employers.

On this particular project, I learned new skills including event planning, customer support, instructional design, creating newsletters, project dash-boarding and end-user training. It was an amazing project and experience, one that was difficult to walk away from. These skills, technology tools and project experiences ultimately led to future opportunities both in and out of industry, such as helping me get accepted into my master's degree program and landing a teaching position in my passion area.

A few other increasingly important skills for you to learn and master include emotional intelligence and focus. First, emotional intelligence refers to the capacity to be aware of, control and express one's emotions and to handle interpersonal relationships judiciously and empathetically. Another way to interpret this is being self-aware of your own emotions, strengths, weaknesses, values and goals and the resulting impact those things will have on others as you make decisions and take action. You are going to have to interact with and often times team up with other people in any business project. Social skills such as motivating others and having empathy are essential in managing relationships to move yourself and others into a desired win-win outcome.

Second, the ability to focus in today's technological driven world full of apps, notifications and text message alerts is becoming a lost art. Can you get through your workday without checking your Facebook, Instagram or Twitter account? How about half your workday? One full hour? If not, then you are not being your most productive self and it will take you longer to accomplish tasks and projects if you allow your time to be consumed by these distractions. While we're on the topic of social media and emotional intelligence, YOU SHOULD ALWAYS BE THINKING ABOUT WHO ELSE MIGHT READ YOUR SOCIAL MEDIA ACCOUNTS BEFORE POSTING OR SHARING. Recruiters and employers will monitor your activity. There are countless stories of people who did not get hired or were fired because of their social media activity. Using common sense will go a long way here – unfortunately there will be other people who will prove that common sense isn't all that common.

I could go on about how learning new skills and taking on new projects ultimately catapulted me to cross the $100K mark throughout my career. By now you have heard enough about the authors of this book. You would probably much rather learn about the career journeys of other individuals who have acquired skills, taken on new projects and have applied their own methods of crushing it in the working world. So if you're ready to be inspired by their own advice, let's dive into the first interview.

Chapter 7: Interview #1
Do the Job of the Per$on Above You

Interview #1

Name: Lou Redwood

Field Studied: Computer Information Systems

Job: Information Technology Security Consultant

Location: Baltimore, Maryland

Reached $100K Mark: Age 26

Interviewed By: Kevin Quinlan

I think that we have opportunities all around us — sometimes we just don't recognize them.

—Lou Holtz
American football player & coach, college football Hall of Fame

What is your background including school, where you're from, what you do, any anything else you can share?

I am from Baltimore, Maryland. I went to James Madison University and studied computer information systems. I graduated in 2009, and then went to work for Freddie Mac in their information technology department. I bounced around in a bunch of different departments, including architecture services, platform engineering and production support. From there I went to go work for Booz Allen Hamilton to do security consulting, so I was on the service-oriented architecture and web service security team for two years with the Internal Revenue Service as my client. I then left and was recruited by Deloitte to go work for their integration engineering service line, but it was essentially security design. I worked there for about eight months and then moved onto Lockheed Martin working with a team where I do IT data center infrastructure security.

Brain Bucks — Notice here we have another individual who reached a great amount of success by shifting around different companies and departments to acquire a variety of skills, projects and experiences.

Did you start working in 2009 or did you have any internships prior to then?

Yes, so I had an internship prior to my junior year in college. I was an IT intern for Freddie Mac and that was the summer of my junior year. They offered me a full-time job before I started my senior year of college to come back and work for them when I graduated.

Brain Bucks — We've already covered some of the benefits of internships for you as the intern, but they are also beneficial to the employer, as they are essentially an extended interview. The company has a longer period of time to evaluate a potential employee. In this case, Lou PERFORMED SO WELL DURING HIS INTERNSHIP THAT THE COMPANY

OFFERED HIM A FULL-TIME JOB BEFORE HE STARTED HIS SENIOR YEAR OF COLLEGE. Imagine what a great feeling it must be to have a job offer in hand before going into your last year of college. YOU CAN GET THOSE EARLY JOB OFFERS TOO, AND INTERNSHIPS ARE THE PRIMARY WAY TO GET THEM!

Would you say it was essential — the importance of that internship to get your career started?

Yeah, I think it definitely helps because everywhere, especially in my career field, the employers want you to have experience. The more experience you have, the better you can build your skill set, which is definitely more valuable in the marketplace. The more skills and more experience you have will definitely lead to more opportunities.

Brain Bucks — Notice a common theme? Many of these interviews continue to focus on building your skills and gaining experience. In the marketplace, this translates to a demand in your services and an increase in salary.

Could you tell me more about the responsibilities at your job?

I work on infrastructure security for government data centers. Essentially, the government contracts out the operations of their data centers and I work to provide security services to them. Day to day is managing security operations, making sure the entire data center is secure. We do a lot of on-call work and deployments as well as security engineering to design systems a specific way to make sure they are secure. There are a lot of federal mandates for how secure government systems need to be, so they have pretty strict guidelines we have to follow.

Brain Bucks — Considering a career in information technology security? The job described in Lou's response is just one of the many opportunities that will be available to you.

Do you enjoy your industry, your responsibilities, and would you say you're passionate about them?

I think I am definitely passionate about my job. I have a very analytical mind, so problem solving and designing things a specific way to solve a real-world problem is definitely something I enjoy. My job allows me a lot of access to systems that touch a lot of people — almost every American, especially with how everything is moving onto the internet.

Brain Bucks — Lou is passionate about his job. Notice the specific skills and responsibilities he mentions that he enjoys doing and how they relate to his job. This is a winning outcome for both Lou and his employer.

Are there any big moves or crucial decisions that come to mind in terms of where you are now and how you got here with your current position and salary?

Yeah, there are definitely things you need to take into consideration. For me specifically, it was recognizing opportunities. You know when you're in a specific job with a specific salary, when you know that your skills are more marketable somewhere else like they always say, "The best time to shop for a new job is when you already have one." So I took the opportunity to look around and see what else was out there. Know the skills and experience you have are valuable — you just have to find the right opportunity. Sometimes getting the interview is the easy part — going in and selling yourself is the challenge.

Brain Bucks — There are a few awesome pieces of advice in Lou's response. First, let's stress the importance of recognizing opportunities. Many people get complacent at their job and don't realize they can go make even more money somewhere else where their talents and skills are more valued. Second, Lou is absolutely right — THE BEST TIME TO LOOK FOR A NEW JOB IS WHEN YOU ALREADY HAVE ONE!

I come from the belief that you differentiate yourself by interviewing when you already have a current job, particularly one you like because then you don't come off as desperate for the job. You might even have some leverage and power in the interview if the company likes your skill set and wants you to come work for them. Whereas the difference with other candidates who don't have a current job, they may try to provide canned answers and what they think the interviewers want to hear. There's really no pressure on you to see what else is out there when you already have something. Do you have any thoughts to add?

Yeah, I totally agree. I think it's very important when you go on an interview to realize they are interviewing you but you are also interviewing the company. When those types of situations occur, usually it's more beneficial for you because if they want you, they have to sell you on them. It's just like those sales meetings — they say, "Someone is always getting sold." Either you're selling them or they are selling you.

What is the fastest way to get promoted within your industry?

Do the job of the person who is a level above you. In my experience, I found you often get rewarded for opportunities or responsibilities that are above your level. You have to search out those opportunities and prove you can be successful at a higher level. A lot of times people think, "Oh if I just work hard in my current role, then a manager will promote me." Usually you have to do something that's above what you think you were capable of to get what you want.

Brain Bucks — Read this response over and over again until it sticks! It is some of the best advice you will receive in this book as it relates to advancing your career and increasing your salary. Lou is absolutely right! Most people work hard, do their job and do it well. However, don't be like most people. Go above and beyond your work responsibilities. WHEN AN OPPORTUNITY ARISES OR ADDITIONAL WORK COMES UP THAT IS ABOVE YOUR LEVEL OR PAY GRADE, TAKE IT ON! You will be rewarded for it and people will take notice. If not, move on to another company where you will be rewarded.

How long did it take you to reach the $100,000 mark?

It took me three and a half to four years to reach that salary.

Brain Bucks — Another professional who reached the $100,000 mark in their mid-20s!

At what point did you realize you had an opportunity to reach this figure for the value you provide?

Mostly when I was looking at marketplace data. When you're in a specific career, talking about salary is pretty off-limits, but with the way things go, sometimes you hear about a friend of a friend who went to a certain company and got an offer for X amount of dollars. So with that information, you can begin to gauge the marketplace. There are a lot of websites you can use to see what kind of pay people are getting for specific roles in certain industries. One of them is Glassdoor.com. But you can go and search for a specific title in a certain area for how much people are being paid for what they're doing and then take it from there and apply it to your industry. They usually provide a general salary range, and if there's an opportunity during an interview, ask for more money — the worst thing they can do is tell you "no."

Brain Bucks — Not sure what your value is? The data is out there. LinkedIn is another resource that has great information. With the advancement of the internet, you should be able to find salary ranges and average salaries for jobs across multiple industries that pique your career interests. You can even add in additional criteria such as education level (degree type) and location to get more refined results that match your criteria. Once you know this information, use it to your advantage during the interview when compensation is brought up by the recruiter.

Was achieving that salary and crossing that six-figure number important to you?

I think psychologically, it is an important number because you realize that you are getting rewarded for the work that you are doing. Salary is the only way companies can show you how much you are worth. You know, they can give you a gold watch or that kind of thing but once you get to that threshold, all of your increases are based on that number, and psychologically it is a huge milestone. I think in your daily life, once you make that amount of money, everything else adjusts up, so it's pretty significant to know that you can go out there and do it.

Brain Bucks — For some people, crossing the $100,000 mark provides a psychological confidence boost in knowing your worth is that valuable to a company in return for the work you are performing.

Do you have any advice you would give to someone who wants to make $100,000 within five years out of college like you did?

Never stop learning. Especially in my industry, you always have to look for new opportunities, even when you think the one that you have is pretty great and you wouldn't mind staying. Looking around is never a bad thing, to know where the market is going — and where you can go to have the biggest opportunity for your career. The best thing you can do is realize when your situation is not conducive to getting where you want to be. Too many times people stay in a company that they are unhappy with for too long — it's a new generation now where company loyalty has gone away and now everyone needs to build their skill set and find the opportunities that are going to better them in their career.

I know that is counterintuitive to what a lot of the older generation thinks. They're the ones who have stayed at the same company for 30 years, but that was back when companies rewarded you with pensions and there was a reason to stay there. Now I think moving around especially with the way technology is, the company is sometimes just a name.

Brain Bucks — Always be learning something but strive to learn something applicable to your career or industry. Sometimes, these large corporations require anywhere from 20-40 learning credit hours per year, and many people rush to find the quick or easy workarounds to check the box when pressed for time. Don't be one of those people — PLAN AHEAD FOR WHAT YOU WANT TO LEARN, TIE IT TO SKILLS YOU WANT TO BUILD OR CERTIFICATIONS YOU WANT TO PICK UP.

Another key point — take a look around you. Is there room to grow and advance in your situation? Are unwritten promises by your boss falling through? If so, it's time to move on! DO NOT ALLOW EXTERNAL CIRCUMSTANCES TO DICTATE YOU STAYING PUT IN THE SAME POSITION OR LEVEL. Many employers can cut back or lay people off with little to no warning. At the same time, you can leave for a better opportunity as soon as you find one, although it is recommended giving 1-2 weeks' notice to keep the relationship intact and leave on a positive note. Company and employee loyalty is not as common as it once was, and it goes both ways.

Are there any obstacles or challenges you had to overcome in order to reach this milestone?

Yeah, I think sometimes managers can get in the way of your achievement. I would not recommend letting anyone else decide your career path for you. You need to decide and take it upon yourself to show that you are ready, and if they are not going to reward you for it, then you need to look somewhere else to find another way to move up. I have had great managers and I have had shitty managers. I have had managers that will fight for you and I have had others that won't fight for you, so you just have to find the right opportunity.

Brain Bucks — Do not allow anyone else to tell you that you can't do something, make more money or advance to the next level. Take action to find the right opportunities.

If you were 22 and just graduated from college, how would you start over, or would you do anything differently knowing what you know now?

I think I would have researched the companies I was applying to. If you are starting your own business, you need to know what you are entering into. If you are looking at a job with a specific salary, you need to know what the company does. Are they going to be around in five years, do they have solid financials? Even knowing that if you are not a financial person — those things are important to you being successful. You need to know everything about the scenario you are about to walk into.

Brain Bucks — Great point! Always do your research on the companies you are applying to and the industries they fall under. Being prepared with this information will reduce the risk of you making a poor career choice.

Are there any "aha" moments that stand out in your career?

Sometimes you realize that the opportunities just aren't there for you to get promoted and it doesn't look like that's going to change anytime soon. What I realized in the business world is everything is negotiable. So when someone tells you that you can't do something, it's because they don't want you to — it's not because you can't do it. My "aha" moment was quitting a company and finding a better opportunity somewhere else that I am much happier with in regards to the job itself, the work-life balance and salary.

Brain Bucks — Contrary to what some people will tell you, do not be afraid to quit a job while focusing in on better job opportunities. Of course, everyone's situation will vary, but searching for a job can take significant energy and time. IF YOU MUST QUIT BEFORE LANDING A JOB SOMEWHERE ELSE, THEN YOU NEED TO HAVE A PLAN TO PAY THE BILLS. You'll need to change your spending habits in the interim and do something to get by.

That is a very different approach from most people who accept workplace complacency and live with the false reality of what they were told on how things were going to be and not put themselves out there to see what's greater. Your thoughts?

Yeah, exactly. Sometimes you can surprise yourself by finding an opportunity that's exactly what you're looking for with the salary you want. It may take some time, but you know sitting around waiting for things to change is usually not the way to go.

Brain Bucks — "Sitting around waiting for things to change is usually not the way to go." This is spot-on true! I've been there as have many others. GO OUT THERE AND GET WHAT YOU WANT. DO NOT WAIT AROUND FOR IT TO COME TO YOU. MOST THINGS IN LIFE AREN'T GIVEN TO YOU.

Did or do you have any mentors, heroes or career role models?

I don't have one specific mentor. I have people that I idolize for their specific skill sets. I had a manager at Freddie Mac I give a lot of credit to. I was with him for a very short amount of time, about six months, but he showed me he was incredibly smart, and had great technical skills and a unique way of problem solving. I think that has gotten me to where I am today. His name was Brian. To think and say, "Well, how would Brian approach this problem and how would he solve it?" Being around those kind of people around is important. I also have managerial people who have really supported and mentored me through, where it's more of a career conversation of "What do you want to do?" "Where do you want to go?" and "What can you do with it?" I had another manager, his name was Ashwini. He used to tell me, "Make sure you know what you're going to do, and make sure there's always room to move up and grow because if you get stuck in one specific thing, then you're not learning anything." So those are the people who stick out in my mind.

Brain Bucks — You can always have multiple mentors to look up to or reach out to in different areas or skill sets. Lou shared with us that he has two mentors he looks up to, one with great technical skills and another with great managerial skills who gave great career advice.

I greatly appreciate your time. All of the advice and insight you mentioned will be extremely valuable to the readers and resonate with them. Thank you.

I think this book is a great idea — a lot of people need to know. Everyone wants to make money but they don't know how to do it. Sometimes applying yourself through things you learn from other people or in this book is the best way to get there.

Chapter 8: Interview #2

The Revenue$ of Law

Interview # 2

Name: Jonathan Turner

Field Studied: Law

Job: Attorney

Location: Orange County, California

Reached $100K Mark: Age 28

Interviewed By: Wes Rowlands

Michael Jordan brings millions of dollars when he shows up in an arena. Since money is how we judge people, he's very valuable.

—Don Yaeger
Award winning keynote speaker, business leadership coach & New York Times best-selling author

What is your background, schooling, training, etc.?

I was born and raised in Orange County, and my parents were both school teachers. I attended a local high school and went on to undergrad at San Diego State, which was literally the only college I applied to. I always had a thought of going to law school even before I applied to college. I guess like a lot of other folks, I read some books about lawyers, watched movies that had lawyers in them, and they kind of got me excited about the occupation. To me, it looked like it was an exciting and lucrative profession. I ended up going to law school at the University of Southern California and immediately went to work for a sole practitioner. Candidly, it was the only job offer I had at the time. I did that for about four years. It was a general practice where I basically participated in all different forms of law. I probably did just about every type of case you can imagine. I did family law, criminal defense and civil litigation, and really found myself enjoying business litigation the most. I just found it to be the most consistent and the best pay, so in the last couple of years at the practice, that's what I focused on. I then moved over to a boutique litigation firm in Newport Beach, California, in 2008 and became partner in 2012 and began working trials alone. Initially the transition to trials without the help of anyone else was scary, but over time, as I took on more and more opportunities, I enhanced my skills and built up a strong client base. Years later, our firm merged with another law firm, and I became an equity shareholder.

I've noticed that since we met many months ago, your passions have evolved. When you started out, were you passionate about your career… are you still passionate about it?

That's a fair question and I think that one of the things people need to understand when coming into this field is that going into the practice of law is exactly what it means — to practice law. Law school is a very intellectual exercise, as it should be. I did not do great in law school — I actually performed just below average. I recognized, however, that I did have the ability to present slightly better than my classmates. This is really important to note, as law is really about being a great communicator. When you are doing litigation, and specifically oral advocacy, it's about communication — stating positions and effectively communicating those positions. Law school, conversely, is more about reading law and analyzing law. It is very cerebral and it deals with a lot of scenarios and in-depth analysis of those scenarios. It teaches you how to understand what a good decision might be in a given scenario and what the best decision might be.

In the practice of law, however, you have paying clients and billable hours that require you to have a certain mentality in business and understanding that you have to be efficient in what you're doing. These environmental factors only exist in the real world, not in a classroom where you are able to just discuss law theoretically. Many people who actually get into the practice of law underestimate the amount of stress that comes along with the actual practicing of law and handling of someone's real case. Very few people are made aware of this stress in law school. One of the best things a law student can do is actually go to work in a law firm. Go get that practical experience — ideally do it before you attend law school.

Brain Bucks — There is no substitute for experience. School can only teach so much, and THERE IS NO WAY TO LEARN ALL OF THE INTRICACIES OF A CAREER BY SITTING IN A CLASSROOM AND STUDYING IT. YOU SHOULD GO OUT AND GET EXPERIENCE as soon as possible so you can find what you like and don't like about a given career field.

As for whether or not I started out passionate, I don't really have an answer. I can tell you, however, that I started out with the love of the idea of being a lawyer. I also loved the idea of being able to impact change. I have since learned that while, yes, the law provides positive change in society, there are many obstacles in the way of accomplishing that goal. It doesn't mean that I have changed my mind necessarily, but it's just the reality. Cases can get very complex and they're constantly evolving, which requires a ton of work. So, sometimes at the end of the case you might question the actual value that was produced compared to how much work was put into it.

You look at the financial and emotional cost to clients, and it's sometimes difficult to recognize whether you are making a difference. I mean, you can see this when looking at the client-attorney relationship. There are very few clients who are happy to see their attorney, particularly when they have been sued. There are many times where the clients just really don't want to be involved in the process. Given that fact, it is such a lengthy process, it can really take a toll on not only the client but also on the attorney. Don't get me wrong, every profession is going to be difficult, so it is important to know that there are a lot of things about the law and the practice of law that are very redeeming. Just know that it is a grind, and you have to adjust your mindset.

I have been in the profession for about 10 years and I have tried over 10 cases, over five jury trials, five arbitrations and bench trials. As co-counsel, I have probably tried close to 20 cases. At this point, having been through it as often as I have been, when cases come in the door, I can pretty much tell the client where I think it's going to end up and what I think they should do. Oftentimes, this just means avoiding a trial and walking away. Very few clients, however, actually want to do to that. They want a fight, and I understand, because that's why we have the process. The clients often feel like they have been brought in wrongfully and there is a principle associated with it.

So I guess where I could see the passion being lost is that I too have gone into it and believed in the principle. Having practiced for a while now I recognize the best result for the client is probably to help them get out of the situation sooner rather than later and not go through litigation — to make an economic-based business decision. I have found that very few people, and even companies, have a difficult time making that decision. So you could see how this dynamic could undermine one's passion because you are counseling against fighting the good fight! You are saying don't fight the good fight, make the good business decision.

So at this juncture in my career, I think if you caught me on a down day I might say, you know what, I know where this case is going to end up, I know that my client is going to have to spend a lot of money, time and emotion, and that litigation is bad for business. I can tell you that at the end of the day, they will likely settle 12 to 18 months from now and they're not going to be particularly happy when they have to settle, so why not get it resolved now? But so few clients are willing to do so, and I completely understand. At that point you find yourself as a litigator, kind of advising against the process because despite the good practical business decisions that the client should be making, they still want to fight. I can tell you from experience, because my day is very busy, the clients generally are not electing to get out sooner rather than later. Of course, there are times where they just don't have a choice to engage in settlement discussions early on.

That being said, having been through all of that experience in all of those trials, and all of that work, there are times when I consider doing something else. I enjoy the skill set of being a litigator, but I've thought about becoming a judge and maybe continuing to be involved in law but from a different angle. Maybe being in a position where I might be able to help people make some decisions and get some resolutions in their cases.

I think you hit on something that's absolute gold in your statement, you mentioned the word "secret." And I can tell you that from my experience and all of my peers' experience, nowhere in school do they tell you if you want to reach the higher levels of any career, in terms of financial success, you better be prepared to bring in business.

Ha-ha, it is definitely the dirty zebra that nobody wants to talk about. At the end of the day it really is a numbers game. What a law firm is looking at is your numbers — the hours you bill and the money you bring in. Those are the only numbers they are looking at, and based on those numbers, they are going to hire and compensate you, particularly as you get further along in your career.

Young lawyers are brought in to do what we would refer to as the "grunt work." They are delegated that work, but if you want to move up in any fashion, you have to (1) be able to send out a bill to a client, have them pay it and send it back, and (2) be able to generate work for other lawyers. That's it! Even when you are interviewing at a firm, they don't ask you how good of a lawyer you are, they don't ask you what cases you've tried — at the end of the day the decision they make to hire you is going to be strictly based on your numbers.

Brain Bucks — If you really want to make it BIG in this field, or any field for that matter, you need to develop the skills of bringing in business — also known as sales! It doesn't matter what industry you are in, businesses exist to sell things, and those people who bring in the sales dollars are the highest compensated.

I bring it up just because it is the absolute reality that students and potential lawyers need to know. For instance when I was in New York City, talking to some very capable managers, the common misconception they all put on the table was they did not realize in order to become a partner and make a much higher level of income, they would actually have to drive in business (money) for the firm. And they said the biggest mistake they made is not preparing for that time when they would actually have to go out and sell and bring in revenue. Now it's kind of late in their careers and they lack the fundamental sales skills they need.

Yes, I would say it is a common problem with the practice of law because young lawyers want to go to large and midsize firms, where they are told to put their head down and work. They are not told that they are expected to bring in business. The problem with this is that putting your head down and working is not is going to lead them to eventually practicing law. Of course doing the work is required for you to continue your career, but at some point, you have to pick your head up and start getting in front of clients and bring in business. That is the only true way you are going to advance. It is the only way you are going to be valued as your career progresses.

When did you first get to $100,000 in salary, and how did you get there?

I was 26 when I graduated from law school, and by the time I was 28, I was making $100,000. This was while I was working for the sole practitioner. In that structure I was being compensated on an hourly rate, I was not an employee, I was paid as a 1099 attorney, so I got paid for the hours that I billed. I think that is the way the typical lawyers would be able to break that $100,000 threshold. But the way I really started to make even more money was when I became responsible for handling my own clients.

To make $100,000 in law, most lawyers can probably go out and find a job that would pay them $100,000. But I think for most lawyers, the more difficult problem is getting past that $100,000 mark. For example, from what I see, it is common for lawyers to practice 20 some years or 30 years or even 35 years, who are still associates at law firms, making $100,000 or $150,000, and that's because they never develop their own book of business. They never figured out how to go out and obtain clients, and that's where you will see people plateau. I remember when I hit the $100,000 milestone, I was certainly happy I was there, but I remember looking around and looking to those attorneys who are at a higher pay scale than me and thinking to myself how can I get to their level?

Brain Bucks — Always be looking up. Once you reach a milestone, whether it be $100K or $500K, always KEEP LOOKING TO THOSE WHO ARE DOING BETTER THAN YOU FOR INSPIRATION. HAPPINESS IS A RESULT OF PROGRESS, NOT REACHING A FINAL DESTINATION.

Did you have any mentors in the process?

I did have one family friend who was a lawyer, and he was someone I would tap into occasionally for information. He probably would've been more available to me if I would've tapped him more, and I probably should have. So if you are a young person and you've got someone who is more experienced in your career who is willing to help you, I would take full advantage of that because they are most likely willing to help you much more than you think. But yes, my mentor practiced law locally, and I went to high school with his son. I don't think I ever necessarily talked to him about business development, but he had a successful practice with a partner, and I could just see from their model that he clearly had his own clients. He was a well-known trial lawyer. This allowed me to see the way I could set myself apart was to go out and try cases.

I took every single opportunity I could to get into court and try a case, which is why I worked for that sole practitioner. When he said, "We have a criminal case," I did it, and when he said, "We have a family case," I did it. I didn't necessarily have an interest in either one of those things, but I knew it presented the opportunity for me to get in court and do trials, so I did it. And I did the business trials when I could, because that's where I wanted to be. But after having gotten all the trial work experience, I could then look at potential clients and say, "I can do this. I have done this. I know what it takes, here are the cases that I've tried, and here are the results that I have obtained." Fortunately those were good results, and it allowed me to get people to start to come into our office and hire me. So that's why I say the experience is so very important.

Getting back to mentors, it's important to know that so many lawyers are actually willing to help. I remember when I was in court and I was there for a trial — it might've been my first or second trial and I didn't have any other senior lawyers at the trial with me. I walked down the hall, grabbed a lawyer on the arm and asked him, "How do I get this into evidence?" He took five minutes and explained to me how to do that. And he said, "If you need anything else just ask me." That was my general experience with law, and I'm sure most other young attorneys would have the same experience. Most lawyers would be willing to help if you just stop and ask them. It's a great idea to get a mentor. It's not something I did a great job of. I do know older attorneys are willing to do it. Just seek them out. Especially older lawyers because I think they identify with younger lawyers and want to help.

Brain Bucks — Find a mentor. Even if you don't know of any mentors right now, like Jonathan, DON'T BE AFRAID TO GRAB SOMEONE ON THE ARM AND ASK FOR HELP, especially those people who have years, even decades, more experience than you.

If you were 22 years old and starting over again, what would you do differently?

I would say take a little more time and actually enjoy it, and absolutely do not be afraid to fail. I would probably go into the practice of law, just as I did, because I think practicing law has treated me very well. I truly do appreciate the skill set I developed from going to law school and for practicing law. Although I don't exactly know what the future of my career holds for me, I do know at the end of the day that I have a profession that supports me and my family if I choose to go forward.

When I was young, I had to take the risks, I had to go out and practice trials even though I wasn't necessarily prepared for them. Some people may say that was brave, and I knew I had fear but I also felt like it was something that I had to prove to myself. That if I made the decision and I want to go to practice law, I had to go out and take those risks. But I also know, in hindsight, that fear of failure did hold me back from trying certain things.

So I would tell young people — you must take risks. Having worked in a profession for long enough now to know that there are going to be cases that I'm going to lose, I know that if I do enough of them I'm going to get great results in the long run. And I should not be afraid of doing things just out of the fear of not succeeding. So as a young lawyer, if you are working hard and keeping the best interests of your client in mind, and you're going in seeking out advice, don't be afraid to take chances in taking on cases. Don't be afraid to try some things. This is probably the most important message I can give to you, to proceed even when you are afraid, because you do not want to deny yourself the opportunity to take responsibility for a case and to see it through.

Brain Bucks — This attorney took a very strategic approach to his career. He noticed in law school that he may not have been good at the typical attorney skill sets, at least by academic standards. He saw the most important thing in being a successful attorney, especially financially, is that he was able to communicate well and that he was actually able to get into trials, which enabled him to acquire clients. Because he focused on those important aspects, he was able to shortcut the entire process and become a very successful attorney.

Chapter 9: Interview #3
Produce the #'$ and You'll Produce Your Own

<u>Interview # 3</u>

Name: Chris Montrose

Field Studied: Hospitality

Job: Mortgage Loan Officer

Location: Philadelphia, Pennsylvania

Reached $100K Mark: Age 26

Interviewed By: Kevin Quinlan

The biggest risk is not taking any risk.... In a world that is changing really quickly, the only strategy that is guaranteed to fail is not taking risks.

—Mark Zuckerberg
Chairman, Chief Executive & Co-founder of Facebook

So let's dive right into it — what's your background, including school, where are you from, anything else you want to share?

I grew up outside of Philadelphia. I really had no idea what I wanted to do. I played a lot of sports and was pretty sociable — I got involved in as much as I could while I was in school — things like student council, community service, those types of activities. I then went away to college at the University of Scranton (Pennsylvania), based off of what I knew about the school because my brother went there. I attended Scranton for two years majoring in business management and then transferred to Penn State University. They did not offer undergraduate business school, so I was deciding to major between hospitality management or health and human development. I decided with having some history of working in restaurants, hospitality might be a better choice. I lost about 18 credits transferring colleges, so I had to pick them up pretty quick. I completed my courses in two and a half years and graduated in December of 2008, which was when the start of the recession occurred. Most of my friends were not getting jobs.

But because I was in hospitality, companies in the industry are always looking to hire. Before that, I had an internship at the Borgata Hotel and Casino in Atlantic City, New Jersey. Atlantic City is pretty much in disarray now with many of the casinos closing. Due to that, they couldn't offer me a job there. I had three job offers and I decided to take a job opportunity close to home because I could save money since I had student loans to pay off. The job was with the Olive Garden, which was not the most ideal job, but it paid the most out of my options. My thinking was that I could live at home, and it paid about $50,000. They gave me benefits, a couple days off during the week. I worked at the Olive Garden for about six months, but I did not like it at all. I did pick up a lot of skills such as managing a group of 50 people, inventory management, ordering, and budgeting. The hours were crazy, and I went to go back to Atlantic City as a job opened up working for Harrah's Casino. I worked there for about eight or nine months, but then realized that hospitality was not for me. Working nights and weekends is tough, and I didn't see growth in the Atlantic City — I just didn't see an opportunity to move forward there.

Brain Bucks — If you end up in a job that you don't like for a period of time, don't disregard the entire experience. MAKE SURE YOU STILL LEARN NEW SKILLS AND TECHNOLOGIES THAT YOU CAN TAKE WITH YOU TO THE NEXT JOB. List them in the applicable sections of your résumé. Always keep an eye out for opportunities to grow and advance.

I began asking around for jobs through people I know, and my friend Dan was working for Wells Fargo Financial, a small part of Wells Fargo. It paid $30K a year plus commission, but they were hard commission goals to hit. I did the interview and bombed it! But I wanted to get the hell out of Atlantic City, so I went to a job fair at the Wells Fargo Center. I saw the same guy I had interviewed with, pulled him to the side and told him, "If you hire me, you won't ever regret it, and I'll produce the numbers you're looking for." He was impressed as he never had someone do that before — so he hired me. I was persistent. I started the job and did pretty well. But it was the subprime mortgage business — it was auto loans that were crazy to sell. They were bringing in 160% loan to value on depreciating assets and credit cards. So it was a tough business. It was working with people mostly right out of college.

Unfortunately, the business unit I was working in shut down, so I signed up to go to Temple University to go back to school for my MBA. But then I got a call the next day from the guy I gave mortgage leads to at Wells Fargo saying, "Why don't you come work for me?" I said, "Well, what's the pay?" It was 100% commission. I told him I couldn't take that risk with having student loans and auto loans. I couldn't afford the risk. But then I talked to my manager, and he thought I was doing pretty well in my role. He said if I take this job, work hard and put in 50-60 hours a week, I'd make $100K. I ended up taking that job and opted not to go back for my MBA.

I got lucky because it was low rates and was with the biggest mortgage servicer in the country, so a little bit of luck was involved. When I wrote my first loan and he showed me how much I can make — I thought that was what I was going do for a pretty long time. The first year I made $100K and the next two years I made around $200K. I was between 26-27 years old at the time. It was a ton of hard work. I moved back home to save money. Because I was living at home, I didn't want to be around my parents, so I would literally go into work early and stay late. The opportunity was there so I did as much as I could with the opportunity. I was there for two and a half years, and then I went to a smaller bank in Philadelphia, and now I'm leaving again to work for a new firm, which is pretty big on the West Coast. They're coming to the Philadelphia market. I'm going to be the branch manager there.

Brain Bucks — Take note of what Chris did here. He was in an unfavorable job situation and TOOK ACTION. He took a chance — he did something most people wouldn't do because it was uncomfortable and requires persistence. He went up to the hiring manager at the job fair with whom he had previously interviewed poorly and promised him performance and numbers. And guess what — he was given a job opportunity that ultimately launched his very successful career. He made the most of that opportunity as well as those that followed while taking a risk of going to a commission-based salary. As you learned from his story, this risk paid off big time!

That's an awesome story. You mentioned that you had an internship with the Borgata Casino. Could you speak to the importance of your internship experience and how it may have started your career?

It was a summer internship with the most popular casino in Atlantic City. It definitely taught me a lot about the service industry and producing a profit on the beverage management side. I had good managers there, but I think another unpaid internship that really didn't count as an internship is when I managed the men's basketball team at Penn State. It is a job I did not get paid for. You work often. It didn't help my grades nor help my social life. It was something I enjoyed because I like basketball. It put a hard work ethic in me — you know doing a job that wasn't enjoyable nor getting much out of it. I think something like that or an internship where you're not getting paid literally will show you the meaning of earning a dollar a little bit more.

Brain Bucks — Another professional sharing how internships were instrumental to his career and how it made him appreciate the meaning of earning a dollar. The students we work with, when the topic of internships comes up, we try to tell them there are some people who think that you should take an internship only if it's paid, which is completely misguided. It's obviously preferable to get paid for an internship if it's the right one for you. However, what we've come across is even if the internship is unpaid, there's a great opportunity in your hands and it's what you make of it. You're already in the door, so at that point you can launch a potential career either at that company or another company after building your résumé.

Could you tell me a little more about your current job and some of the responsibilities that you have?

Sure. So it's a 100% commission-based job. A lot of it is about relationships. It's the mortgage business. I originate loans but it is basically sales and selling yourself. Meeting with financial planners, realtors, title representatives and attorneys. Being personable, reliable, answering the phone on the weekends and at night. Being available for your clients. It's not easy, if you read online about it. It is a tough business and there's a lot of paperwork. I take the client from the beginning to when they're ready to buy a house. Even clients who aren't ready to buy a house who have bad credit, I will take them from that point all the way up to buying a home. Then staying in contact with them if they ever want to refinance, buy another house or if they have a friend buying a house. It is very important staying in contact with your past clients for future business.

Brain Bucks — You never know when a potential lead or customer is going to instantly make the switch to become a current customer. Notice Chris stressing a reoccurring theme — THE IMPORTANCE OF RELATIONSHIPS AND STAYING IN CONTACT WITH ALL POTENTIAL LEADS, PAST CUSTOMERS AND CONTACTS. This increases his business and that increases his salary compensation.

Do you enjoy it and would you say you are passionate about it?

I do enjoy it. It can be stressful, but I think anything you're going to do making money is stressful at some point. The reason I do enjoy it is you take someone and help them buy their biggest financial asset. It's a pretty big thrill when someone buys their first house or helping an investor get an investment property. I was able to build off of that, I began buying investment properties, so I have four of my own. I have seen how other people are successful doing that. You come across places that are great investments and make money that way as well. Also, it's fun to go out and meet people. You go to a lot of events. I try to put myself in the Philadelphia real estate market as much as possible by advertising, going to charity events and telling people what I do — people have to know what you do in sales.

Brain Bucks — Two things here. (1) ALWAYS KNOW YOUR "WHY" — IN THIS CASE WHY YOU ARE PASSIONATE OR ENJOY DOING WHAT YOU DO FOR YOUR CAREER. Knowing it will put you at ease and motivate you to get up every day and do your job well. (2) DON'T EVER HESITATE TO TELL PEOPLE WHAT YOU DO AND HOW YOU MIGHT BE ABLE TO HELP THEM OR SOMEBODY THEY KNOW, especially if you are in sales. It exudes confidence and people otherwise won't know — you will miss out on opportunities to increase your compensation.

That's really interesting. You mentioned something earlier which I want to come back to because it was an incredible story. You spoke of how when you went to a job fair and you walked up to the hiring manager at Wells Fargo and told him that you will make the numbers he was looking for and that nobody will work harder. Seems like a gutsy strategy and clearly, it worked for you. Would you say doing that or anything else was a big move that got you to where you are now?

I don't know where I would be if I didn't do that. But also I think going with your gut on decisions to make money is huge. I think there's risk involved that comes with everything if you want to make money. I think transferring colleges was a big risk. Leaving the industry that I studied for was a big risk. Going to a job with a 100% commission-based salary was a big risk. Buying properties has been a big risk. I'm leaving the current company I'm at right now, and I'm not going for the safe choice. I'm not going with a big bank — I'm going with a lender that has no presence in Philadelphia — but I think it's the best choice for a long sustainable career. I did my research on the company. It's a huge risk but that's all I've been doing in the last couple of weeks. When you have multiple offers, you really have to do your research and call as many people who don't have skin in the game as possible.

Brain Bucks — Crossing the $100K mark usually involves taking risks. It's important to evaluate the risk and take some on but never blindly. Always do your research whether on the internet or speaking with others, including mentors and those already in the industry or working for the company.

What would you say is the fastest way to get promoted in your industry?

Returning phone calls and emails in a timely matter, being available and putting in the hours.

At what point did you realize you had an opportunity to reach what we call the $100K threshold for the value you provide?

Probably the first time I wrote a mortgage loan and saw how large the opportunity was. If I worked hard and put the time in, this was something that was definitely attainable pretty quickly. Not everyone has that opportunity, but I saw it and ran with it.

Brain Bucks — Note the reoccurring theme of hard work. Sounds simple enough but it's the truth.

How long did it take you to reach the $100K mark in your salary and compensation?

So I graduated in December 2008, and I hit $100K by the end of December of 2011. That was at the age of 26.

Some people associate a certain level of success with crossing that number. Did achieving that particular salary mean anything to you when you first did? Or was it like, "It's nice, I'll keep going?"

It was definitely a good feeling because I was so young. But also, with the mortgage business, the rates were very low at the time, so I didn't know if it was something that was sustainable. Because I was only doing refinances, my manager said, "You have to get into the purchase market." I was doing 90% refinances and now I'm 90% on the purchase side and that's basically because I saw the writing on the wall and put in the work in order to sustain that income level. I'm not currently where I was with regards to compensation in 2012 and 2013, but I think this year I could get back to that number. I'm around $130-140K now. I could get back up to $200K next year. We'll see.

Were there any obstacles or challenges you had to overcome in order to reach the $100K milestone?

You have to know your priorities. You're going to miss out on some things, social gatherings with family and friends at times — especially early on. But once you've established yourself, you can make more time for that. The stress level can be a little high. In my role, I'm dealing with someone's biggest financial asset and things don't always go right. A lot of paperwork is involved. I can be on the receiving end of a lot of shit. Another big one is overcoming the fear of commission.

Brain Bucks — Hard work usually comes with shifting around your priorities and making sacrifices. PUTTING YOUR CAREER AT THE TOP OF YOUR LIST OF PRIORITIES WILL INCREASE THE ODDS OF YOU BEING SUCCESSFUL.

That's interesting. Being full time on a commission-based salary has got to be pretty scary the first time.

Yeah, especially when coming out of college with student loans. But I just have a theory that if you're not going to school to be a doctor, lawyer or your family has a business for you to make money, you might as well be an entrepreneur, which my job technically is. You know, being in sales or being an entrepreneur is pretty much the most direct path of getting to $100K. If you take a $40K or $50K-per-year business job, banking job or something equivalent, it's probably not going happen as fast. You can do that for a couple of years, but it's probably going take a while until your mid-30s to get there.

Brain Bucks — While there are multiple jobs and industries where you can reach the $100K mark, it is true that one of the fastest ways to get there is having a pay-for-performance structure — usually it is based on sales or revenue you bring into the company or business.

It's interesting because a lot of people I've talked to in sales — what I've come to learn is that it's the #1 skill anyone can learn, and some people

think that they can get away from it in other industries. **For example, I know a few lawyers — they have a very good base salary, but where they really are going to crush it is making it as a partner by bringing in revenue and clients into the firm.**

Next question, if you were 22 and just graduated from college, would you do anything differently knowing what you know now?

Yeah, I would have gotten into what I am doing now right away! I would have bought investment properties in distressed areas that seem like they might go up soon. I think I'd be a multi-millionaire now if I bought in places that were struggling a bit that are better right now. Some of those properties are now in huge popular areas that are going off in the Philadelphia market. I would've done that. I would've taken chances earlier. I wouldn't have messed around and stayed in that college lifestyle as long as I did.

Brain Bucks — We continue to hear people saying they wish they had learned more about finance and real estate and invested earlier. Take some of your free time and learn these essential areas. You will know more than the majority of people who choose not to learn these topics and will be more able to recognize great opportunities when they present themselves.

Are there any "aha" moments that stick out in your career?

Yeah, seeing my boss being the first one into the office and the last one out at Wells Fargo. Another one would be taking care of the people who refer you business and then seeing them give you even more business back again. I also went to a life-coaching seminar with Tony Robbins a year ago — I think that was really good.

Did you invest in that personally or did you get some assistance from your company?

My company.

What a great opportunity.

If you could do something like that, do it as early as possible. If you do it earlier, it's better. I wish I went to it eight years ago.

💵 *Brain Bucks — Couple of key points here. (1) WHEN YOU'RE THE FIRST ONE INTO THE OFFICE, YOU WILL BE SURPRISED HOW MUCH WORK YOU CAN GET DONE BEFORE ANYONE ELSE STOPS BY YOUR WORK SPACE, EMAILS OR CALLS YOU. These are all unplanned interruptions that take time away from your list of goals and tasks of daily accomplishments. As an added bonus, being one of the first into the office looks really good for you when you are being reviewed by your supervisor for a raise or promotion. (2) Always take opportunities for meaningful professional development, coaching or training workshops, especially if your company is going to support it through paid time off or reimbursement.*

Additionally, some companies provide full or partial tuition reimbursement for you to go back to school and get an advanced degree. TAKE ADVANTAGE OF THESE OPPORTUNITIES — IT IS ESSENTIALLY FREE MONEY! An advanced degree can help lead you to making more money with your next job opportunity.

Did you have any mentors, heroes or career role models along your journey?

Yes. My current boss and then my old boss at Wells Fargo. Even though we battled — I respect him and he put the work ethic into me by being able to see his example. He taught me how to work hard and be the first one in and last one out of the office every day and put the hours in over the weekends. We always stay in touch. My current boss taught me the Philadelphia market and introduced me to a lot of people. He got me involved. Wells Fargo was more of working hard with the leads that came in and putting in the hours. My current company, with being on the purchase side — it is more focused on putting yourself in social environments to build relationships and taking care of people who take care of you through referral partnerships. They're both very successful — and taught me both sides of the business.

Brain Bucks — A good role model or mentor in the working world doesn't always have to be someone you are close to or a friend with but can be someone you admire or respect.

What is the best way to take care of people who send you business?

Handwritten notes are good. A simple lunch, a simple dinner. A Christmas gift. Showing them that you care. If you can ever send them some business, you do it. Answering their calls and emails in a timely manner.

Brain Bucks — REFERRALS ARE CRUCIAL FOR YOU TO SUCCEED. It all comes together in this interview. Build relationships. Foster those relationships over time. Help people by working hard for them. The REFERRALS WILL COME IN OVER TIME AFTER THE VALUE PROVIDED TO YOUR CUSTOMERS HAS BEEN PROVIDED. Take care of those people by the ideas Chris provides, and if you can ever return the favor for someone else, do it.

Chapter 10: Interview #4
De$ire to Know More Than Anyone Else

Interview #4

Name: Tina Nelson

Field Studied: Computer Science & Mathematics, M.B.A.

Job: Technology & Delivery Consultant

Location: Everywhere — she works where her clients are

Reached $100K Mark: Age 29

Interviewed By: Wes Rowlands

The more you read, the more things you will know. The more you learn, the more places you'll go.

—Dr. Seuss
American writer & illustrator

I used to work with Tina and have a ridiculous amount of respect for her. Not only because of her skills but because of her general philosophy about work and life. She is incredibly hard-working, and it really was an honor to work with her. I know you guys will learn a ton.

Could you tell us about your background, schooling, training, etc.?

Sure, I have an undergraduate degree in computer science and mathematics from a pretty reputable school in Waterloo, Canada. After graduating, I worked for a couple years as a developer and went back to school to get an MBA. I didn't really specialize in anything during my MBA, as I wanted be a generalist and try to learn different subject areas. Post MBA, I did a short stint at the Ministry of Health doing some policy work. I then decided to move into consulting and now I work for a consulting firm specializing in the technology and delivery phase within the financial services industry. I have been there for about four years now and it's been great.

What do you like about your job, and are you passionate about what you do?

I am definitely passionate about my career, otherwise I wouldn't have lasted as long as I have. I have a mild form of ADD (Attention Deficit Disorder). If I'm not passionate about something, I'm not going to stick around.

What do I like about it? I think part of the reason I joined consulting is because of the change of pace and change in projects you get to work on. So it doesn't necessarily mean that you're always working on a different subject area, but it's always interesting to be working with different clients and learn about the relationships you have to build or the dynamics you have to work through to deliver what you need. I think that in itself can motivate you, keep you interested and maintain passion for your job. I think that's what keeps me in it — my need for constant change and the ability to work on different projects, with different clients, in different subjects areas. That's been what driving me.

However, the fast-paced constantly evolving environment, while it keeps me engaged, is a double-edged sword. I travel a lot, which initially was interesting and fun, but it does drain you. I think traveling every week is like a drug. Today you could be in New York City, three days from now in Chicago and next week in Scotland. Always meeting new people, experiencing new places, eating at different restaurants every night — it becomes addictive but it can be detrimental. The tough part is finding that balance of how much can you do and stepping back and figuring out what's more important in life. And to be honest, I am doing a lot of introspective analysis to create what I want the next phase of my career to look like.

That makes a lot of sense. I have had a lot of conversations offline with you specifically on that topic. What you are going through is very consistent with a lot of people we interview — that your career is constantly an ebb and flow of emotion, and I think that's kind of the name of the game — at least from what I can gather not only from my own experience but from talking to people like you.

So if you had to put your finger on it, what are some crucial moves you made in your career? Are there any key deflection points in your career you can point out?

Definitely. One of the key points in my career when I started out early in consulting, and Wes, you were a part of it because you were on the same team as I was. I think I started as a business analyst, which was my initial role on the project. I was a pretty junior-level member of the firm, but I think what made me successful was being self-aware and wanting to do more and know more than my specific job.

Brain Bucks — KNOW AS MUCH AS YOU CAN! Set a goal to be the most knowledgeable about your job, your department, your company, your industry, and you will put yourself miles ahead of your peers. Of course, this takes a lot of time — years even, but it is worth the effort.

I think that's what got me to where I am right now as fast as I did. I'm not the type of person who just does what I am told. And that's part of what makes me successful. I am passionate about what I do, so if I have an opinion, I will voice it and will make sure it's heard. I'm not the type of person to be pigeon-holed into a role. So if I am part of a large program, I don't just pay attention to what I am doing, I'm also mindful of what's going on around me and I want to know how it affects what I'm working on. Having the desire to learn constantly and wanting to know more than what I've been told to know is what's gotten me where I am right now. I think that first project where I really made a difference was because I took the initiative to learn more and demonstrate not only to the partners that I work with but also to the clients how valuable I am because of the skills I bring to the table, such as the ability to learn quickly and maneuverer to the different areas of the business and the stakeholders.

Now I think what you're hitting on is really profound, and I want to take a second here just to point out a key concept that I was taught a long time ago: IF YOU WANT TO GO FAR IN AN INDUSTRY, WORK HARDER ON YOURSELF THAN YOU DO ON YOUR ACTUAL JOB. And that sounds counterintuitive, but I think you're hitting that same vein, which is you're going to get a list of things to do during the day for your tasks, and that's going to fit into eight hours, but the reality is if you only check the boxes on those basic action items for the day and don't put in the extra hours to learn more, then you've got no shot at advancing. After working with you personally, I know for a fact you were putting in three, four, five, six hours a day EXTRA while other people were not willing to put in that same effort.

I think you just hit the nail on the head because if you only work for eight hours or only do what's expected of you, you're going to have the average trajectory that's set out for you. You're going to be part of the norm — you're not going to be the exception. There's a career path that is set out for everyone when you join a firm. There's a path set out for you by society or by the industry that implies you work the eight hours. You put in your time and then you maybe get small promotions every now and again, but you will never make huge leaps in progress. If you don't go the extra mile to do something different to stand out, you are signing up for a mediocre career.

That makes a ton of sense. So what would you say is the fastest way to get promoted in your industry?

Demonstrating value to your clients and to your firm. We don't have one skill we look for — we look for someone's ability to be diversified in their skill set and the ability to quickly think and adapt in different situations. Our employees must have an analytical mind that can assess what to do in a given situation, react in the right way, and deliver what is needed to the client. That's what makes you successful in consulting. It's not about a specific skill set that you learn in school. Academic knowledge does help you, but I think in order to be a successful consultant, you need to have an awareness of your surroundings and be able to adapt appropriately to a given situation.

A large portion of these interviews are focused on teaching readers different career paths and also pathways to financial success through those careers. There's a tremendous amount of content out there that pushes "Follow your passion and don't worry about the money." I actually disagree with this philosophy. You should follow your passion AND also be focused on making the money. Because at the end of the day, if you're doing something you're passionate about but it's not paying the bills, you will quickly find out that's a formula for unhappiness.

That being said, let's talk about money. At what age did you start making $100,000 a year?

Within two years of finishing my MBA, I was 29 years old.

Was that a big benchmark for you or did it just sound more glamorous than what it actually was?

I think you start to lose sight of that $100K number as you get closer to it, sadly. It was a benchmark when I started my MBA and I also had a benchmark of what I needed to make in salary for the expense of graduate school to be worth the investment. Essentially within three years, my salary increased so much that the cost of my MBA was paid for.

Brain Bucks — It's essential to SET YOUR BENCHMARKS AND YOUR MILESTONES, BUT JUST REALIZE THAT THESE ARE GOING TO BE MOVING TARGETS. What you think is a lot of money today, trust me, five years from now will not be what you think it is. That's just how psychology works. And as your income grows, your needs will all of a sudden grow as well.

Tina, if you were to give advice to somebody who wants to excel as quickly as you did, what would you say to them? In other words, if you were giving advice to your younger self — let's say you were 24 years old, knowing what you know now, what advice would you give your younger self?

I'd say, simply — work hard. It goes without saying but it's one of the things that I start to see less and less of in younger generations unfortunately.

Brain Bucks — Good old-fashioned HARD WORK. IT'S A CONCEPT AS OLD AS TIME, BUT HARD WORK NEVER GOES OUT OF STYLE. When in doubt, keep working harder! Don't know the next step to take in your career? Put in the work to figure it out. Need to make more money? Put in the work to earn a higher paycheck. Want to get promoted to the next level? Work so hard your bosses notice and can't help but to put you in a leadership seat.

I would also recommend to constantly learn about your industry, your job and pretty much any education you can get your hands on. To that end, don't just learn about the job you're doing, but learn what other people are doing, learn what other departments are doing. I think that's important and will help you figure out what you want do and where you want be five years from now. I would also advise to always put effort into discovering what makes you happy and to be passionate about what you do.

Reflecting back on your career, did you have any "aha" moments?

I was kind of naïve when I came out of the MBA program. I thought I wanted to work in the public sector. Just as a warning to the readers, the public sector is for people with a certain personality, and it works for those people in some cases. I was naïve enough to ignore all of those warnings and think that I could make a difference, which was very important to me because at that time, I wanted to do something that made an impact on society.

I waited a long time to get into the public sector and eventually landed a 13-month contract but quit after six months. I had that "aha" moment where I knew I wasn't cut out for it and I knew I wouldn't last in the industry working at such a slow pace and being immersed in an environment where nobody wanted to grow or be challenged. It's all about being self-aware and knowing that despite your best intentions, you have to do what is in line of what drives you. Despite me wanting to work in the public sector to give something back, I knew I couldn't be passionate about it, therefore I couldn't be happy with what I did.

It's really funny of you to bring that up because obviously you and I worked a lot together and just knowing what I know about you, I'm laughing in my head thinking — *holy crap! If Tina were to work in the public sector, there is no way in the world that would be sustainable!* And for the readers who may not understand, I'm kind of reading between the lines here, but I see Tina as a very driven, hardworking, passionate, multi-curious type of person. The public sector, from at least from my experience, does not have many people like Tina.

Absolutely, that is what drew me away from it. I went in there because I was passionate about making a change and having an impact, but I wasn't able to accomplish that goal. I gave it my all in the six months but quickly became very frustrated with not being able to influence any changes. Like you said, I am a driven person and I do like to see progress. I like to see the value of my work and I like to see the fruit of my labor, and that just wasn't happening for me in the public sector.

Brain Bucks — Sometimes you have to change course. There's a difference between quitting and pivoting. Quitting is stopping because you don't want to put in the effort. PIVOTING IS STRATEGICALLY ALTERING YOUR COURSE BECAUSE THE PATH IS NOT LEADING YOU TO YOUR DESIRED DESTINATION. ONLY YOU CAN DECIDE whether you are quitting or pivoting.

Did you have or do you have any mentors along the way?

Very good question. People have always asked me this question, and I don't have any official mentors. But that doesn't mean I don't go to people for advice, as there are a few trusted people I will talk to every couple of months to give me a sense of direction. If I'm struggling on a project or I need advice on how to deal with a client or situation, there are definitely people I go to for input. But what I don't have, and probably should start looking for, is a consistent mentor I can speak to about my career path and my life goals. I sort of plan peripherally around what is happening in my life, but I do consult with people I trust and who have opinions I value.

That list of people includes a couple of people from the firm I work with, a couple of professors and family members who have helped me along the way. It is a variety of people. It is important not having just one mentor because you need different perspectives. If you only talk to people in the same industry, you might not get the right perspective. Whereas if you have a wide variety of mentors, it will give you a different view of life.

I just want to point out something to everybody, and Tina if you don't mind me commenting because you're too humble, tell me to stop. Tina has reached a very high level of success, very early in her career, and it's not a mistake. If I were to deconstruct the evolution of her progress and look at the individual elements that make up her entire character and her reputation, I see somebody who has earned a degree in a very technical background in mathematics and computer science and then capped off her

academic career with an MBA. On top of that, she is incredibly skilled at communicating. And finally, the fact that she is a female, something that is statistically unlikely in technical fields, makes her an extremely rare person in the workplace, especially in the financial services consulting world. Tina, would you say that's a fair assessment?

Yeah, absolutely it is. I don't often speak of it but when someone does point it out, then I realize, yeah it's true. I am usually the only female at a senior client meeting or even at a discussion in our firm. We have a technology practice and I'm definitely the only person at my level who is a female. So yeah, I don't often consciously think about that but it is definitely one of the things I had to work through. I don't want to say "overcome" because that makes it sound dramatic but it's definitely something I had to work at. Even throughout my undergrad career, I earned a degree where I did an internship every other term and I was the only female on my team most of the time. It's something you learn to adapt to early on in your career as a female technologist, and you have to quickly learn how to be heard in a male-dominated industry.

Brain Bucks — It pays to be different. Maybe you're a female, like Tina, in a male-dominated industry. Maybe you're the youngest person in your company. Maybe you come from a different background than your co-workers. Whatever the case, INSTEAD OF VIEWING YOUR DIFFERENCES AS WEAKNESS, VIEW THEM AS THE STRENGTHS THAT THEY REALLY ARE, AND CAPITALIZE OFF OF THEM!

Chapter 11: Interview #5

In $ales, the $ky Is Your Limit

Interview #5

Name: Zach Bedford

Field Studied: Hospitality & Tourism Management

Job: Marketing Associate (Sales)

Location: Washington, D.C., Area

Reached $100K Mark: Age 25

Interviewed By: Kevin Quinlan

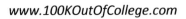

It takes courage to grow up and become who you really are.

—E. E. Cummings
American poet, painter & author

What is your background with schooling, work experience and your career?

I went to a public high school for four years, graduated and initially went to college in North Carolina to play golf. I was big into golf during high school. I thought I wanted to play golf in college through a professional golf management program but ended up taking a detour. After some introspective analysis I discovered that I enjoyed the game too much as an activity and passion but didn't want to make it a professional career. After I had that epiphany or whatever you would call it, and I transferred to James Madison University in 2004 to major in hospitality and minor in human resource development.

I have always been interested in the food industry and was told by numerous people I would be a good salesperson. I didn't really know where I was going to go after college, but I got a job as a wine salesman with a company called Associated Distributors to gain some sales experience because the end game was to get a job with Sysco Food Services. I needed to have sales numbers and experience to prove to them because they were a large, top 50 company. I couldn't rely only on my good looks, ha-ha.

Brain Bucks — I'm sure most of you at one point are asked, "What do you want to do when you grow up?" or "What do you want to do with that degree after college?" Truth is, most people don't really know. It can be an overwhelming and deeply rooted question for many people.

You may not know what you want to do right away or in five years from now, but you should start to figure out "WHAT IT IS YOU WANT IN LIFE" — from all angles and categories. Start with the end goal in mind and work backwards.

In this case, Zach focused and spent time researching and learning about both himself and the industry. He had a dream job (sales) and dream company (Sysco Food Services), which he knew he wanted to work for in the future. That was the end goal — from there he determined and executed a plan of how to arrive at his goal by first landing a job with a company that would provide him with the sales experience he needed to get to Sysco. He then took action and put in the work to become a successful salesman. Within a few years, he was working at his dream job.

YOU CAN GET TO YOUR DREAM JOB TOO, BUT THE STARTING POINT IS KNOWING WHAT YOU WANT — YOUR PURPOSE AND YOUR END GOAL.

Did you start working in the industry you're now in prior to your job with Associated Distributors?

No, my first job was when I was in eighth grade — I worked at a college dining hall. Way back in the day on Saturdays and Sundays working brunch flipping pancakes, French toast, washing pots and pans — it was a terrible job. But my parents tried to instill a good work ethic in me at a young age and show me the value of money and all that. So I did it and worked at the golf course growing up all through high school and once I transferred back to JMU, I worked at the Joshua Wilton House (fine-dining restaurant), so I served in the industry which at times can be "sales-like" but never directly on the sales side.

Brain Bucks — We all have to start out working somewhere. Sometimes these positions or internships are not "sexy." What we say to that is: WHO CARES?! If the job or position can be tied to the industry you are interested in pursuing, then go after it! Just the experience alone should be worth it for a spot on your résumé and a topic of conversation during interviews. You also will begin to grow a network of people who may be able to help you right away or know someone else who can. Make the most of your time, work hard and get to know people. As you have already heard and will learn about in these interviews, many job offers come down to who you know. We can't emphasize it enough — get to know people and get them on your side!

120

Could you tell me what some of the responsibilities are on a typical day at your job?

Yeah, it's pretty much juggling fireballs. I mean you have a list of tasks of what you hope to accomplish that day, but the industry that we're in with Sysco, it's very hands on and human interactive and can change quickly. So when I meet with a customer to give me an order, I then transmit the order on my computer. I'll say we need 100 pounds of salmon fillets, 300 pounds of chicken, etc. I then transmit the order and it goes to our warehouse and it is then picked up and operated all by humans. Human error is a big part of it, and with transportation operations, trying to get the order complete and to come full circle can throw a few wrenches into my system every day.

I have a set task list of what I hope to perform every day whether it's seeing a prospect, trying to get a new customer, seeing the customer to talk about a new item for an upcoming event they have going on or trying to keep the competition away from my current customers. In the food world, which is different than the wine world, we all sell the same thing, so you have to differentiate yourself in terms of how you're selling your product. In the wine and beer world, you have the rights to the products, so customers come to you. Whereas in the food industry, you have to go to the customer and keep them happy.

Brain Bucks — How many times have you gone to class or gone to work and when the day was over ask yourself, "What exactly did I get done today?" Sometimes we cannot remember and other times we may have allowed unexpected tasks or interruptions to take over what we initially planned to accomplish for the day. Being aware of this is essential towards your production output and results.

Zach practices a great habit here, and while it sounds simple (it really is), many people do not make this a routine practice. EACH NIGHT BEFORE YOU GO TO SLEEP, SET A TASK LIST OF WHAT YOU PLAN TO ACCOMPLISH THE NEXT DAY. This should include what you plan to accomplish with your classes, with your job and in your personal life, such as going to the gym or buying that birthday card for Mom.

Do you enjoy your industry, job and responsibilities, and would you say you're passionate about them?

Yes, I would. I mean I've always wanted to have my own restaurant, but now being in the industry, I get the best of both worlds. I walk around the place, get to hang out in the kitchen and talk to the general manager, talk to the owner, pretend like I'm part of the team without having to deal with the headaches and the late nights, hourly employees, people calling out and trying to steal from you all the time, which is probably the biggest problem in the restaurant industry. But yeah, I enjoy it. I'm passionate about it. I mean food is my passion both at home and professionally, and I do enjoy helping people succeed and get that gratification when a chef is looking for a certain product or something that he's never heard of. To be that consultant for them to show them here's a new idea, a new item, that we have to instill the relationship and show my services — that I'm not just there to sell him or her another case of chicken wings.

Brain Bucks — Find your passion! Zach's passion was working in the food and restaurant industry. He was able to enter it by using his knowledge of food and his skills (sales and customer service) to get exactly what he wanted. Because he is working in his passion, he looks forward to getting up in the morning and being successful at his job and for his clients. NOBODY, REGARDLESS OF WHERE THEY WENT TO SCHOOL OR HOW SMART THEY ARE, CAN COMPETE WITH SOMEONE ELSE WHO LOVES THEIR JOB. If you don't love what you do, then eventually someone else who does love it will pass you by.

What were some of the big moves or decisions you made along your career that got you to where you are now?

Well technically, I'm still in the same role that I started in about five years ago with my current company. But the change of companies was a big jump for me in my career. When I was at my previous employer, I wanted to move my career forward and apply to be the district manager of the Northern Virginia team. But I don't think I was chosen for that job due to my few years of experience because I had only been there for a year and a half and I was 23 years old at the time. There were grown men and women on this team, and I think they were afraid I would not be able to lead them, given the fact I was much younger than they were.

I think a lot of it, as we were talking earlier, was just pure dedication. You are pretty much given a small territory when you start, you kind of have to build it on your own. You're sort of your own entrepreneur. You have the backing in funds of a large corporation but you're kind of out there on your own trying to create relationships and have prospective clients become customers and to go through the selling phase. I think the hard work and dedication in the beginning showed senior management I was passionate about this, had the drive and was going to be successful — that I wasn't going to take "no" for an answer. That led to me gaining more customers when certain people would leave or get promoted. Additionally, if I had to be honest, a lot of it was having a personality, which fits well with customers. I'm easy-going, laid-back and always looking for a good time, so it just seemed to work with a lot of people.

Brain Bucks — For those of you interested in going into sales, this is an excellent outlook and approach on how to view your role. While you may work for a company, you are largely working for yourself when on a commission-based salary. You make money for the business you bring in, similar to that of an entrepreneur.

What's the fastest way to get promoted within your industry?

In the sales industry, it's always about "What did you do for me today?" As terrible as that is, it's a numbers game when it comes down to it in the end. Yes, you're a person and you have your style and all that, but with sales it's always about the numbers. So if you are up, you are in the green and growing from last year's numbers. You are looked at differently even though you may not be doing anything different. In terms of promotion or growth, some people stay in sales at the associate level for their entire career, while others go into management. It all depends on what you want personally and what your short-term, mid-term and long-term goals are.

Brain Bucks — Read over that last sentence in Zach's answer. We touched on this earlier in the book but it comes up again in this interview. Take an hour or two and DETERMINE WHAT YOU WANT OUT OF A CAREER AND SET SHORT-TERM, MID-TERM AND LONG-TERM GOALS. THEN ACT ON THOSE GOALS.

How long did it take you to reach the one $100,000 mark?

I started out at a base salary from day one. My goal after talking with fellow coworkers and my mentor seemed to be about three to three and a half years — that is the point where you hope to get your territory to a large enough size and hit that $100,000 mark. So based on my hard work, timing and a little bit of luck, I completed that at the end of year three. At my company, after you start bringing in a certain amount of sales per week, you are on a 100% commission-based salary, so the "sky is the limit." You could make as much money as you're trying to make. I have just tried every year to make more money than I have made in the previous year, and so far I have been successful in doing that.

Brain Bucks — Notice the common themes that keep reoccurring in what it takes to be successful: hard work, persistence and a little timing or luck. We've already touched on hard work and being persistent. Let's take a closer look at the timing and luck component. While it is true that sometimes catching the right break can get you to that next level, I would argue that Zach and every other successful person we have interviewed who mentions "timing" or being "lucky" have CREATED THEIR OWN LUCK BY PERFORMING THE HARD WORK, PUTTING THEMSELVES IN GOOD POSITIONS AND BUILDING KEY RELATIONSHIPS.

Did achieving that salary mean anything to you — was it important to cross that exact figure?

Yeah, it did mean a lot to me given that I thought I would never achieve that milestone. It was even more special to me since I hit the goal at such a young age. At the same time, once I got there, I wanted to reach a higher level of income — I guess that's just human nature. In sales, the well is endless, so really, you can make what you want, as long as you are willing to work for it. For me, I always want more, so I continually want to do better this year than I did the last.

Brain Bucks — Here's a great piece of advice to those who reach the $100,000 mark: KEEP GOING! Don't get complacent — be hungry and find ways to grow. This growth will usually be associated with an additional increase in your income.

What advice would you give to someone, regardless of their industry, who wants to make that kind of money within a couple years out of college?

You have to be a team player, you have to prove to your management that you're an asset to the company. I remember my parents always told me growing up, "Find what you love, and the money will follow." I think kids of our generation feel entitled and say, "Well I graduated, so you should pay me $95,000 out of college to sit here and do whatever." You know the real world is a tough place, and that's not always what happens. You've got to toe the line and play the game. There is a lot that goes into financial success, but being a team player and working hard are probably the most essential components. Being dedicated and having an open line of communication with your current boss to make sure everyone is on the same page are crucial ways to career advancement.

Brain Bucks — Great piece of advice offered in this response. In most jobs, you will have a boss who you meet with on a few occasions during the year. One of those meetings will be to discuss your goals, accomplishments and next year's compensation. The key here is to do exactly what Zach says — HAVE AN OPEN LINE OF COMMUNICATION ABOUT YOUR PROGRESS, ACCOMPLISHMENTS AND WHERE YOU STAND AGAINST YOUR GOALS. Meet at least every other month as a check-in meeting with your boss. This will ensure a HIGHER PROBABILITY OF EARNING A COMPENSATION INCREASE OR BONUS AT THE END OF THE YEAR, as your boss will be constantly aware of your progress.

If you were 22 and just graduated from college, would you do anything differently to get to where you are now?

No, I don't think I would. I took a pretty direct but smart path to get the job and career I wanted. I knew I needed sales experience if I wanted to work for a larger sales company, so I found a company that would let me do that out of college making $35,000. You know it was tough, putting your nose down, grinding it out, creating a budget and living a little bit more frugally. I realized my short-term pain would be a long-term gain. I just tried to exceed my previous numbers and blow the roof off the original place. When you're 22 years old, you are just nowadays hoping to get a job. If I could do it over again I would go into the information technology industry, given the large amount of opportunities available.

Internships are huge now too, even if they are unpaid. Companies like to see that you have worked in a professional environment at a young age, taking the responsibility to differentiate yourself among the hundreds of thousands of college graduates.

Did you have any internships?

I interned at Marriott. I actually worked in the sales office right outside of their corporate headquarters in Bethesda, Maryland. It was an eye-opening learning experience because I got to see what corporate America is like and how certain things work. It was a nice little token on my résumé when meeting with prospective companies to take a job on, especially graduating out of college. My hospitality program required you to have a 400-hour internship during the summer between your junior and senior year, and you're like, "Come on, this is the last hurrah," but looking back on it now, it was a great experience and got me to where I am today, so I am very thankful for it.

Brain Bucks — His internship experience gave him a leg up on his competition for jobs with prospective employers. Key takeaway — get internships!

Are there any "aha" moments that stick out in your mind from your career?

For me personally at this company, at Sysco, it is a tough gig. It is a seven-day-a-week job, 365 days a year. Restaurants are most busy from Friday night through Sunday afternoon when you are hoping to spend time with your girlfriend, friends and family, so having that balancing act has been difficult, but it does come easier with time.

The "aha" moment for me occurred about a year and a half into the job, when I realized you have to be a consultant to your customers and take pride in their business. If you're just doing the job simply to check a box, it's not going to work. Really caring about all of my customers is what really set me apart from my peers in the industry. I share my passion with them, I want them to be successful because if they are successful and growing, then I am growing as well.

Brain Bucks — Every job has its challenges. Take a step back and realize things come with the nature of the job that you may not enjoy 100% of the time. Zach's industry can call for tough and unexpected hours, but his passion for the job gets him through this challenge.

GENUINELY TAKING PRIDE IN YOUR CUSTOMERS, CLIENTS AND PARTNERS' BUSINESS IS AN INCREDIBLE OUTLOOK FOR ANYONE who works in customer service, sales or any profession where you are dealing with people. These relationships are vital to your success as well.

Did you have any mentors, heroes or career role models along your way?

Obviously my parents and grandparents played huge role in developing me as a well-rounded person, but when it comes to business, one mentor immediately comes to mind, Clark Murray. Outside sales can be a challenging job especially when you are speaking with chefs who are high-tempered, impatient and could possibly be under the influence of drugs or alcohol. With sales, you can get rejected all day every day, making it feel like you're getting kicked while you're down. It can be exhausting. It was during those really low times that my mentor, Clark, would lift up my spirits and motivate me to keep going. I was so lucky to have him by my side as a coach. He was one of the best in the industry, probably the top guy in our entire company. He really took me under his wing and showed me what needed to be done to be a successful sales associate. He worked with me for four years and just moved on last November.

Another facet of my life that was crucial in building my sales skills was the game of golf. I was a young kid at 14 or 15 years old playing golf with grown men — you know they really don't respect you because they think you're just out there ruining the game. Once you show them that you're there to be serious and to actually play the game and beat them, they start treating you with a little more respect and showing you some things. It gave me a good jumpstart on life — talking to people and strangers when you're 15 trying to create conversations with 45- to 55-year-old men and women. You learn to be quick on your feet and have those conversations. So I would say those are my mentors and what's made me the person who I am today.

Brain Bucks — One of the most important decisions you will make in your career is deciding on having a mentor and determining who that person will be. Mentors can often act as a sounding board and be a strong influence by offering invaluable advice based on their experience. While it takes some time to create a mentor-mentee relationship, don't hesitate to reach out to a highly trusted family member or friend for immediate advice.

Chapter 12: Interview #6
Bring More Value than Your Co$t

Interview #6

Name: Joe Harper

Field Studied: Actuarial Science, Mathematics and Statistics

Job: Actuary

Location: Philadelphia, Pennsylvania

Reached $100K Mark: Age 26

Interviewed by: Wes Rowlands

You don't get paid for the hour. You get paid for the value you bring to the hour.

—Jim Rohn
American entrepreneur, author & motivational speaker

Joe, what is your background in terms of schooling and your occupation? What is your story?

In high school I took a bunch of math classes because I was interested in the subject. I excelled at math and kept moving higher in the curriculum — AP calculus, AP statistics, etc. I then went on to study math for my undergraduate degree. After several internships during college, I went on to work full-time for an insurance company, and I've been working there for the last seven years.

What was your first internship, and how did you get it?

I got my first internship through an internship career fair held at my university. I knew landing an internship was going to be pretty competitive, so I came prepared. I did my due diligence ahead of time and targeted any companies that were in the Philadelphia area because I wanted to stay relatively close to home. From there I wrote cover letters and I created my résumé, which I tailored toward each company. As result, because of the extra detail and effort I put in, I ended up getting interviews, and one of them ended up turning into an internship.

As an important side note, I even attended the internship career fair as a freshman, even though I knew I wouldn't land a job. I always encourage freshmen to do this even though they're probably not going to get a job, but it at least helps them practice talking to companies.

Brain Bucks — Preparation is key! Notice how Joe started preparing for an opportunity (in this case, he attended a career fair as a freshman) well before he actually needed it. Too many people trying to become successful wait until the last minute to seek out opportunities, when in reality, waiting will only guarantee those opportunities will pass you by.

How did you pick the direction of the career you wanted to head into?

Well, I was always good at math, so I guess I originally thought I would be either a teacher or an engineer. But then one day the guidance counselor at my high school talked about actuarial science. She described what an actuary was, and it was fascinating to me. When I was looking at colleges, I was looking with both engineering and actuarial science in mind, and Penn State had that combination, so I thought it was a good fit. When I started out in college, I was in enrolled in the College of Engineering for chemical engineering but I was also taking insurance courses as well. In my sophomore year I ended up switching to actuarial studies from engineering.

It was actually kind of by chance that I found out about actuarial sciences. I was a math major in a pure sense, but if you are a math major, that's traditionally more of a teaching major, although there is a ton of applied math that I would encourage people to do. Plus, if you major in math or engineering or anything similar, you are not necessarily going to apply what you learn but at least you learn how to think and practice logic. For example, there are a lot of engineers who don't end up going into engineering. They will end up going into finance or somewhere else, but they come away from an engineering degree understanding how to think and solve problems. So yes, part of it was chance, part of it was just homework and taking action once I heard about becoming an actuary. I did my research and saw for instance, that an actuary was one of the top five occupations listed in the *Wall Street Journal*.

That's an interesting point. I remember reading one day that Steve Jobs said everyone should learn how to code a computer, not necessarily to become a computer programmer, but to actually learn how to think.

I completely agree. I actually regret not taking a programming class in high school. But I did take a full coding course in college and learned some through others. But yes, learning how to code even at a basic level is awesome.

Getting back to my first internship experience, it was a great program the company had. It was held at an insurance company, and it was incredible, in the sense that they actually gave me real work. There are definitely some internships you get that don't really give you a ton of applicable work but give you a bunch of busywork. For example, just getting coffee for executives, making copies, etc. Instead, this company had a decent model for internships that they separated into four goals:

1. To see if the intern likes the company and the industry

2. To see if the company likes the intern

3. For the intern to get real experience

4. For the intern to make money

The company made out on the deal because they essentially got a summer long job interview where they could see if they wanted to hire you full-time.

You hit on a really interesting point when you said that your internship was a great experience because you were not doing busywork. We run into this issue a lot with students, where they are afraid to get an internship because they feel like they are only going to be doing minutia, such as making copies. But what most students don't realize is that even in that worst-case scenario, doing busywork is way better than the alternative of not having an internship. Just being in the door and gaining exposure to the work environment, having opportunities of projects that come up and so on, is way worth the experience. Would you agree?

I absolutely agree, and there are so many things that you don't learn in school or a textbook, that your first internship forces you to learn. I remember just learning things in Microsoft Excel, email etiquette, scheduling a meeting, and other things that you will never learn inside of the classroom. There are a lot of intangibles that are learned during your first internship, even if it is not your dream internship. And, although this may sound counterintuitive, the intangibles are what have to be learned, as they are often what will hold you back in a company. For instance, even if you get hired straight out of college into a great job, a lot of those intangibles will be a barrier for you to make progress early on in your career. For example, if you have not already had the experience of say, making copies, setting up meetings, or doing any of that basic elementary stuff. Even if you do cover some of it in school, it's usually just a one-time project or something of a similar nature. Whereas a lot of activities we're talking about here, you have to do in the workplace many times a day.

Brain Bucks — EVEN IF YOUR FIRST INTERNSHIP IS NOT GLAMOROUS, IT IS STILL WORTH IT, AS YOU WILL LEARN ALL OF THE FUNDAMENTALS (THE INTANGIBLES) NECESSARY TO PROFESSIONALLY CONDUCT YOURSELF IN THE WORKING WORLD. There is no shortcut to these types of real-world lessons, so get the experience as soon as you can!

My second internship was done at the same company, and I worked for them during the winter break as well. I came back for my second summer internship, and I ended up on a different team in a different department. It was a different experience, but it was also cool because I found myself learning every day at my job, which should be everybody's goal. I worked as hard as I could, and it paid off, as the company gave me a full-time offer, which I ended up accepting.

So what do you do for your full-time job now?

I am an actuary, which in general means I discount cash flows, perform analysis and help the company make decisions. For instance, I help perform calculations for pricing of insurance products, as there are going to be certain premiums and claims against the policies that the insurance company creates. In other words, I have to help the insurance company figure out how it should price the policies it creates to ensure they are profitable. It is an actuary's job to recognize the patterns and different embedded options.

Through mathematical modeling, we also look at things like worst-case scenarios, best-case scenarios, etc. Basically quantifying all risks to a company, and then making decisions based off of that information. To give more detail, when an insurance company sells a product, a certain amount of money has to be set aside. If someone gives you a premium of $100, you can't claim all of that $100 as profit. You should probably put a lot of it away to pay for future claims. So what is the appropriate amount to set aside? In actuarial science, we figure out that answer. There's a whole valuation area that specifically deals with these types of issues. This is more tied in with balance sheets, the income statement and other types of accounting.

Another area of actuarial science is called risk management where you would be looking at assets and liabilities of the insurance company and looking at ways to manage risk of the company's policies. Once a policy is sold, it could be on the company's books for many years. Given this type of business structure can become quite complicated, there are entire teams dedicated to analyzing these policies. They are looking to see if there are any sort of trends happening or decisions to be made based on the company's "book of business."

In terms of my most recent transition, I just moved into the investment side of the business. Although actuarial science and investments tend to have some parallels, they also have many differences. Actuaries deal with liabilities, and the investment world deals with assets. They do a lot of similar things as far as modeling and looking at cash flows, but they don't speak the same language usually, so there can be a lot of communication difficulties. This is understandable, as any business has its own acronyms and most businesses have lots of them. I'm just getting used to this new role. It is difficult even to have a simple conversation, as communicating with veterans of any industry can be challenging as a rookie.

Have you historically and do you presently like the skills you have been using in your career?

I have always liked the skills I've been using in my professional career. In addition to sharpening my skills of being an actuary, I also ended up acquiring management skills through leading a team about three years into my career. Although I was not expecting this type of responsibility, nor did I really eagerly welcome it at the time, it ended up being a great experience. The role gave me insight into what is expected of managers. As entry-level employees, we tend to not appreciate how much is expected of our bosses. We tend to only see one side of it, which is just work getting delegated to us. But then when you are put on the other side of the table, it really opens up your mind. What I have found is going in with the mentality of serving the people you are leading is the best leadership style that you can adopt. If your employees are happy, they will work harder for you. The other thing I really appreciate about the insurance company I work for is they have a rotational program, so I got to learn about different areas of the company and also work with a bunch of different teammates along the way.

Brain Bucks — *RECEIVING MORE RESPONSIBILITY IS PART OF THE GAME WHEN INCREASING YOUR SALARY TO $100K. Just like Joe, when you are stepping into a role that expects more from you, it is not going to feel comfortable at first, but if you stick with it and work hard, it will all be worth it!*

Are you passionate about what you do?

Yes, I really like math and applied math. I get to use math every day to help solve real-world problems. Working with insurance is really fascinating because the nature of the business is very probabilistic, which is why actuaries are very much in demand. Creating models and deconstructing problems are pretty great skills to have. I do feel fortunate to be able to go to work and to get a chance to solve those problems and continue to learn.

Do you think it is essential for you to like what you do?

You have to at least like what you do, and it is preferable you love what you do. In order to be an actuary, there are series of actuarial exams you have to pass. There are about nine of these tests depending on how you count, offered about twice a year. Each test requires roughly 300 hours of study, and the exams vary from three hours to six hours. It is definitely a lot of sacrifice in college. I remember when I passed my first three exams in college, it was really helpful to have classes that covered some of the content of the test. It got a little difficult during my fourth exam because my school did not have any courses to help me with that material. I had to go out on my own and do an independent study. This essentially meant I had to prepare on my own. I would not go out on Friday nights when the rest of my friends were having fun and partying. It became quite socially difficult. Although it was challenging at the time, I look back on it now and I am thankful for having done this early in my career. I've noticed when other people try to do it later on in life, for example a career changer, the transition can be even more difficult, especially if you have a family.

Are there any big moves or pivot points in your career that put you at the next level?

I think the biggest thing is just hard work. I grew up as an athlete, on some very competitive teams — that really helped me in my career. Knowing the simple concept that if you want to get better at something just practice it repeatedly and you should get substantially better. It's the same thing in your career. Being an athlete also helps you understand the big picture, deferring enjoyment for now for a larger future benefit is very much worth it.

Another thing that really helped me on the way was being a tutor in college. I tutored all eight semesters in college. The whole idea of "teach something to master it" is spot on. Being forced to teach the material I had to learn was incredibly helpful to me. Passing actuarial exams early on was also another catalyst for my growth. This strategy helped me to get internships early, which is what allowed me to get an offer before I went back to school my senior year.

I would also say that strategic planning really helped me advance my career pretty quickly. For example, when I went to college I studied the syllabus of the curriculum and figured out that I could configure my classes in a certain way that would help me advance quicker than my peers. By doing this, I was able to take the more advanced actuarial classes when I was a sophomore in college, whereas usually you have wait until your junior year. I remember I built a pretty detailed spreadsheet to help plan several semesters in advance. Not only did this help me advance beyond my peers quickly, it also gave me the freedom in my final college semester to take classes that I enjoyed.

While we are on the topic, I would definitely say that planning and preparation were absolute key for me. I noticed a lot of people I went to school with planned poorly, and they ended up really paying the price. They had to cram in really difficult classes during their final semesters, and it did not yield great results. I would definitely recommend planning whenever you can, and getting ahead of the game whenever you can. Even if it means taking some summer classes or an extra class early on, do whatever you can to get ahead.

Brain Bucks — STRATEGIC PLANNING IS NECESSARY FOR SUCCESS. Think about your goals. Constantly be asking yourself questions such as "Where do I want to be in five years?" Then, THINK THROUGH THE ANSWERS AND WRITE THEM DOWN. Going through planning sessions for all areas of your life will pay huge dividends for your future. Do this process often, as life is continuously changing, so you have to repeatedly make sure you are on the right track.

What is the fastest way to get promoted in your industry?

Passing exams, as there are different raises and promotions associated with passing them. For my particular company, there is definitely an emphasis on both doing well in your career and also passing the exams at the same time. If you are just passing the test but your work is not sufficient, that's not going to cut it in the long term. There's also something that's happening right now in the industry, which is students coming out of college having already passed six exams.

And there's a big debate going on in the industry because employers are questioning how much is too much in terms of academic advancement, over actual career experience. So you have a lot of the students graduating with a bunch of tests under their belts, but they don't actually have the experience of working for a company. Regardless of how many tests you pass, at the end of the day what matters is the value you provide to the company, and the most viable person is the one who has proven it through experience. Experience is something that cannot be taught; it can only be gained over time. Of course, once you are a credentialed actuary, it definitely helps advance your career. For example, once you are credentialed, you're able to sign off on certain things. It usually enables you to lead inside of a company in certain areas, and in general it sets you up to be in a good leadership position.

When did you hit the $100,000 salary mark, and did you have any thoughts or emotions tied to this number?

I was 26 years old. As my salary grew, I definitely had some mental hesitation along the way. Because as you grow up, you really only have a handful of data points to recognize what is a reasonable salary for people. And the more you are paid, the more anxiety seems to come along with it. Questions arise such as "Am I worthy of this price?" I had seen in my company different restructurings where people were fired, and you could reasonably conclude that some of the people were let go because they were making too much money — they were too expensive for the company. So I do tend to have thoughts every now and again that make me a little concerned about making more money. Obviously the money is nice, but there is a little hesitation, as it might increase my odds of being let go. To help combat against this mindset, it is always helpful to put to paper some projects you've done that can be related to tangible revenue you've either brought in for the company or have saved the company to justify your salary.

There is a guy on YouTube I watch who has a great point, which is if you want to make money, then you have to produce more value for a company than you're being paid. If a company, let's say, is paying you $10 an hour, you have to produce more than $10 worth of value to the company or else they're not going to pay you, because it won't make sense. I would definitely recommend that every employee adopt this healthy mindset. In other words, the best way for success when working inside of any company is to bring in more dollars than you cost.

Brain Bucks — BRING IN MORE MONEY FOR THE COMPANY THAN YOU ARE BEING PAID, AND YOU WILL HAVE A LONG, SUCCESSFUL CAREER. If you really want to execute this well, use the "follow the money" principle. Look to see where the money is made in the company, and work in that department or position. For instance, all companies make money through selling products or services. So, if you want to stay close to the money and prove that you help bring in money for the company, either become a salesperson or be the creator of the product or service.

Did making $100,000 a year change your life in anyway or change your mind set in anyway?

I don't really think so as I'm not really that frivolous. I don't think many of my friends, for example, have any idea how much I make currently, and I like that. I don't need to show off how much money I make through the shoes I wear, the vacations I go on or anything materialistic like that. Instead what I do and what I would recommend others do is live below your means, invest a lot of money, and give to charity.

Brain Bucks — Earn as much money as possible, spend very little of it, invest, and give to charity. Simple!

What were the defining characteristics of your journey that advanced you quicker than your peers?

When I originally started on my career, a percentage of my job was related to the stock market. Instead of just doing only my job, I made sure I went incredibly in-depth to understand the financial models in this area, probably more than anybody who worked in the company. Basically, I didn't only learn the "what" and the "how to do things" in this particular job, I learned how to answer the question of "Why?"

In the world of finance, there's an incredible amount of data and things that get spit out of financial models. It is a very large task to even understand those outputs. Most people just stop there and that's fine, but I wanted to go further and understand why the results were what they were. This enabled me to go back to my boss and not just report on what the numbers were but WHY the numbers were what they were. When you adopt a strategy like this, it gives you a deeper level of understanding, which ultimately produces better work.

The way I did this in my career was by simply going through a ton of spreadsheets and looking into the actual computer code of the models. I looked at the whole system from front to back. Of course this takes a ton of time, but it is definitely worth it. If you can do something similar in a new job and become the go-to person who is the expert, you will be valuable on all levels at your company. For anybody who is trying to excel at their job, if you are given a task, don't just complete that task or push the buttons or whatever the elementary level of execution would be, really take the time to get into the details.

Don't get me wrong, committing to understanding the company or the complexities of the business in its entirety is incredibly time-consuming and frustrating at times. You often do not even realize the fruit of your labor, at least in the short term. However if you keep on working at it, you will eventually come across an "aha" moment when you are able to connect the dots of how two things you didn't understand were related. If you keep working hard at it, you all of a sudden know more than everybody else around you.

So how did you become the subject-matter expert in different areas of the company?

Well, I always let my curiosity lead to side projects of the major project I was working on. So if I ever had a project where I didn't understand how it all worked, I would spend the extra hours to really do the research myself to make sure I understood it completely. As a side note, I would also tell people who are trying to get promoted, to have a goal of making their boss look good.

Follow the cash. I had a finance professor when I was in college tell me that if I want to be successful in my career, to follow the cash. Meaning that if you can understand how your company makes money and you can add to that money, you will learn how the company works, probably more than most of your peers, and you will also become successful at your career.

What obstacles did you hit in your career, and how did you overcome them?

I failed some actuarial exams several times, which was very frustrating but humbling at the same time. It is certainly not a fun experience when you spend so much time studying, giving up on all the parties and other social things you could have been doing and then you still fail the exam. Trust me it's not a good experience at least initially, but in the end, if you keep on pushing forward it ultimately helps you learn more about the content and helps you develop a stronger character because you were willing to overcome adversity.

From your experience, what would be the quickest way to earn $100,000 in a career?

Well, that's a really difficult question, because I do think before you enter into your career you should really evaluate and think about what you are good at and what skills you have. For example, if somebody is very creative and artistic, they probably should not become an actuary because by its very nature, an actuary is very formulaic — pretty much the opposite of creative.

With that being said, if your goal is to make $100,000, it's probably going to be a result of working at something that you are good at as well as what you are passionate about. They are not always the same. You could be really passionate about something that you are just mediocre at or you could be really good at something that you're not very passionate about.

So if you had to do it all over again, would you do anything differently?

I don't think I would do anything differently. Maybe I would learn coding more because I do feel like the world has changed since I've graduated college and is changing even faster now, to being more coding centric. But other than that, I don't think I would change a thing. I get to learn new things every day, which I think is extremely important in anybody's career, so I'm always being challenged and always being forced to grow.

Did you have any heroes or mentors along the way?

There were definitely several senior actuaries in my company that I have continued to look up to for guidance. Having people in my industry who I could always go to and count on for advice has been instrumental to my success. Additionally, I've always looked up to my father for business advice. If I ever encounter a situation where I need to think through the business side of things and really look at it from a different angle, I always go to my father. I read a lot of business books to help fill in knowledge gaps, and I am a devout Catholic, so I read a lot of books about inspiring saints, philosophy and theology.

Any final tips for the readers?

Be sure to always work hard and constantly acquire in-demand skills. I would definitely advise people to learn another language. I don't remember the exact statistic, but I think I've heard that on average, people who know two or more languages earn roughly $150,000 more over their career than people who don't have a multilingual ability.

Brain Bucks — Always be sharpening your saw and adding new tools to your belt! In other words, always be making progress. PROGRESS IN YOUR EXISTING SKILLS AND ADDING NEW SKILLS THAT ARE MARKETABLE IN YOUR INDUSTRY. Find a list of the top skills necessary in your career field (do this by asking people or just plain Googling it) and get to work!

Chapter 13: Interview #7

From "0" to $ix-Figure Tech Pro

Interview #7

Name: Michael Freeman

Field Studied: Computer Information Systems

Job: Data Architect (Business Intelligence)

Location: Northern Virginia Area

Reached $100K Mark: Age 25

Interviewed By: Kevin Quinlan

Surround yourself with only people who are going to lift you higher.

—Oprah Winfrey
American media proprietor, talk show host & producer

What's your background?

I was a James Madison University '09 grad — computer information systems major. The big thing about CIS is that people don't realize is it's a half business, half computer science major. So we took classes like the management, accounting, and the College of Business courses, which put us through all the basic management, operations, marketing and finance courses. Then we had the computer science part of it as well, so I took a programming course, a database course, a software lifecycle course, which I think put me in line to be a consultant because I can talk to people about their business and I also know the background of IT.

When did you start working?

In 2009, after I graduated. We did on-campus recruiting with Freddie Mac, so I was right out of college. I started two weeks after I graduated.

Did you have any internships before you started your career?

I had two internships. I did not get either internship through my college. I applied to a few, but I had a poor GPA so I didn't get selected for any. I actually found two random internships when I went home for the summer; one I found on Craig's List — I was browsing for part-time jobs and a company was looking for a junior network engineer, so I just applied saying, "Hey I don't have any experience, I don't even want to be paid, would you be OK with me coming in?" They said, "Most definitely." They were completely cool with it and I learned a lot there because there was no structure — it was a sales firm. Everyone was just constantly berating people about getting their computers up and running, getting the network up and running. If anything went down, people were losing money because they were all working off commission. So I kind of learned by being thrown into the fire there because everyone I was learning from was constantly in the fire.

Brain Bucks — Amazing point of information here. Michael realized he did not have a great GPA, so he had to rely on himself to go outside the university to gain internship experience. He showed determination and creativity by conducting his own research, reaching out to companies and setting himself apart from others by being open and informing the company he wasn't concerned with getting paid. He demonstrated a willingness to learn and gain experience.

IF YOU ARE HAVING A DIFFICULT TIME LANDING AN INTERNSHIP, OFFER TO WORK FOR FREE! The short-term pain (of not getting paid) will bring you a long-term gain in the form of experience, credibility and future opportunities when the money gets more serious. By the way, some employers have to pay their interns by law or company policy, but offer to work for free anyway — you will stand out from your competition!

Can you tell me about your second internship?

The second internship I did was through one of my mom's friends. Her son worked in IT and my mom knew I didn't have an internship at the time, so she asked if I could shadow him since she knew that was the direction I was going in. He did basic help-desk support, so I worked as an intern there doing basic troubleshooting work.

Brain Bucks — This is a great example of using a relationship (friend of the family) to shadow a professional in your desired field to gain an internship experience. An INTERNSHIP EXPERIENCE DOES NOT HAVE TO BE STRUCTURED to be considered a legitimate internship.

That's awesome you found something on Craig's List of all places and offered to put yourself out there and work for free. Would you say those internships were instrumental in being considered by employers out of college, given your other qualifications?

Yeah, most definitely! I mean when we did the on-campus recruiting, there is not a whole lot to talk about. There are only so many behavioral questions you can answer like "Tell me a time you struggled in a group and came together." But talking about *actual work experience* helped me a lot moving along those interviews because if I have a résumé where I am a pizza delivery guy, the only thing we can talk about is my school work. But the fact that I can bring these internship experiences to the table and say, "Hey, I did this...." and it wasn't even in technology that I ended up going into but just the fact that I had a real-life example and not college group work made a big difference!

Brain Bucks — Notice here that Michael immediately knows the value and importance of his internships. They brought him real-world skills, knowledge and project experience that he was able to speak about at the interview table. This helps expedite the routine behavioral interview questions and dive into his value demonstration of work he has already performed. INTERNSHIPS ARE THE FOUNDATION OF YOUR CAREER PATH TO GET YOU TO THAT $100,000 JOB FASTER.

We've come across many employers — a lot of people think they care what you can do for them and that's true but they're more interested about what work you have already performed in the past. Do you have any thoughts on that?

I agree with that, especially at the beginner level as most people don't have great experience coming out of college. Even the people I knew that interned at Deloitte or one of these big companies, they did the same thing I did at my internships. Again, it was just the fact that I can talk about some sort of work experience and see how I can think on my feet, that's what the companies are looking for. They are not looking for an expert in X technology at that point. They are looking for people who are intelligent and can pick up things on their own.

Brain Bucks — For entry-level positions out of college, employers are looking for internship experience, how candidates can think on their feet (whether they are trainable), intelligence and versatility — meaning you have the ability to work independently but also work collaboratively in a team environment.

Could you tell me what you currently do, what your day is like and some of your responsibilities?

I'm a data architect. I work in a very narrow field of data Architecture as well as government consulting and business intelligence. Business intelligence is a gigantic field right now, but it's also a field where not everyone knows exactly what it entails. So there is kind of two ways you can go about business intelligence. It's the analytics and that's the machine learning, all the people finding patterns — looking at things and all the really cool buzzwords like "big data" — that's what I consider the cool side of business intelligence. Then there is government business intelligence, which is just dash-boarding, making reports, and all it entails is presenting data in a different way to higher-ups (senior management level personnel and above) in a way for them to make decisions.

So for me, I understand business intelligence solutions because I've worked on so many. My background is data migration, so these companies have a thousand different systems that they've bought over however long they have existed, and business intelligence is coming in and trying to combine all of that data because a CEO, chief technology officer or chief information officer is not going to go look at all the different systems — he or she wants to look at one spreadsheet or one graph and make a decision off of that consolidated information.

So my first job involved getting the data out of these systems and putting it into one central system for these business intelligence tools to come in and report from. Originally, I was working for a data architect who was working with a bunch of different tools and business intelligence solutions, and he knew what things should look like. All he would tell me would be to go to a specific system, grab a piece of data and put it here in our system, and I would develop processes that accomplished that objective. As I moved through my career, I've seen a lot of these solutions before, so now I am the one who says, "Hey, I know the BI solution will pick-up data faster if we put data in this way, it will work out better." So now that I have seen 10-15 different solutions because *I've worked on multiple projects*, I am the one who is designing these backend databases that the BI tools use. Now I am the person who tells people the process to grab data and move it to the right place in the system.

Brain Bucks — As you see throughout these interviews, gaining experience WORKING ON MULTIPLE PROJECTS IS A GREAT WAY TO BUILD YOUR SKILL SET, GAIN EXPERIENCE AND INCREASE YOUR VALUE to a company in exchange for higher compensation.

What would you say you like about the industry and your job responsibilities, and do you feel passionate about them?

So that's a loaded question. From personal experience, I do not enjoy working. The thing is, if I did something else, I don't think I would like it any more. I like problem solving — so when I get a new issue, I love the first few hours or day or however long it is for me to go in there and design a solution to solve the business' problem. The issue for me is all the other stuff that goes along with it. It's an hour of fun but then seven hours of error checking, fact checking, meetings with the client and dealing with their bullshit and other things I find boring. I enjoy the problem-solving part of it, and no matter where I'm going to work, there's going to be that other part. So the fact that I at least have that hour of fun is what I like about it. The funny thing is I thought it would get better as I move throughout my career, but now it's not better. It's just different. I think it's just me personally — I don't think I'm going to enjoy 100% of my time working no matter what I do.

Brain Bucks — Take note that Michael knows exactly what it is that he enjoys doing at his job and what he does well. THIS IS WHAT EVERYONE NEEDS TO FIND IN THEIR JOB AND CAREER IN ORDER TO ACHIEVE LONG-TERM SUCCESS. He also knows the things that he does not like doing at his job. However, what Michael should constantly strive to do is find a way or role that allows him to spend even more time problem solving and designing solutions since that is his passion within his line of work.

What were any big moves or crucial decisions that enabled you to get to where you are now with your salary?

I have taken a very odd route because I am five years out of college and I'm on my fifth job. Every single interview now is not about "What you can do anymore?" It's kind of a small world — people know who I am especially in this industry and they ask, "Why should we hire you if you're going to leave in eight months?" But the decision for me to leave every company I have left was the right decision for me because there are not that many 27-year-old data architects in the world. You become an architect because you see a ton of solutions. Because I left so many companies and have worked on so many projects, I have seen so many different things and different technologies. So I have the experience now to say, "Yes, we are going to do something this way because I did that at XYZ Company, and it worked." Leaving that many companies in a short time span is not something I would suggest, but at the same time it has worked out in my favor. I've enjoyed working at all of the companies I have been at except for one as well as the people I have worked with, but jumping around has worked out better for me and my career.

Brain Bucks — There is more than one way to $100K. Michael did it by doing the "5-5-5 Deal," and we're not speaking about Domino's Pizza in this instance. He hopped around five jobs with five different companies in five years. While he openly admits that he wouldn't recommend doing that for everyone, he recognized in each case it was the right career move for him. His self-awareness of this is essential as he has to anticipate interview questions about this frequent movement from employers and alleviate their concerns with well thought out responses about his short-term tenure at past companies.

You said there aren't many data architects out there. As you were considering career moves, did you realize what your value was to the marketplace?

Most definitely. Do you know what DICE is?

No.

DICE is like the Monster.com for information technology jobs. You go in and enter your skill level, and a thousand jobs pop up. For example, if you go to the site and type "Java programming" — every junior-level position populates. Seeing that helped me realize the jobs that were out there. I was lucky — I didn't choose my first position, I got hired by Freddie Mac, and they told me, "This is what you're going to be doing." As I started to learn more about it, I realized there are not many people who do this — and thought this is awesome. I am in demand in this field, this is great. I just kind of ran with it and recognized that business Intelligence is huge but still small in the government space, which is what I wanted to do.

Brain Bucks — Michael realized the experience he was gaining and skills he was learning had a huge demand, but there weren't many people doing business intelligence work in his specific niche area. He did his own research and realized early on what companies would be willing to pay for someone with these skills. As a good practice, FREQUENTLY CONDUCT YOUR OWN RESEARCH TO SEE WHAT SALARIES PEOPLE IN SIMILAR FIELDS, ROLES AND LOCATIONS ARE RECEIVING. Having that research and information in your back pocket come review or interview time will help give you the ammunition needed to negotiate a higher salary for the value you provide.

How long did it take you to reach the $100,000 mark in your compensation?

When I left my third company for my fourth company at the age of 25.

Brain Bucks — Michael reached the $100K mark in year three out of college!

Did achieving this salary mean anything, crossing the six-figure mark? Was it a goal of yours?

It's kind of funny, when my friends and I started working, I had no sense of what salaries were. When I was offered my first salary, I said, "I think that's good." The people who were around me which I believe is a big part of the reason where I find myself today told me, "We should be making $100K by the time were 25." I thought they were being ridiculous but when I left my first company for my second company and received a 25% raise, I started to think that maybe this was doable! After that moment, I always said, "All right, $100K by the time we're 25, let's do it." I ended up hitting the $100K mark one month before my 26th birthday, but that wasn't the reason I switched companies. It just happened to be the right career move at the time. It was always in my head, but I don't think it ever drove me — it was just about getting what I felt I deserved to be paid.

What's the fastest way to get promoted in your industry?

For IT, I think it's leaving. Honestly, especially around the D.C. metro area, IT is all about the technologies you know and if you sit on your ass and stay at one company, you're not going to learn any new technology. That's the whole thing. In IT, they want smart people. They don't really care what technology you came from, it's about how you're going to pick up the next one.

That's incredibly insightful.

Brain Bucks — In this career field, Michael KNEW EXACTLY WHAT EMPLOYERS WANTED TO SEE — SO HE CREATED AND EXECUTED A CAREER PLAN DOING JUST THAT, a versatile path of mobility where he was constantly learning new technologies (skills). Once he mastered one, he moved onto to the next company to learn a new one — each time resulting in earning a higher salary on the road to making $100K!

What advice would you give to someone who just graduated from college and is looking to make $100K within several years?

The biggest thing for me was living with and speaking to friends in my industry. None of us were competing with each other, but it was always a friendly rivalry. When my one friends left Freddie Mac for Booz Allen Hamilton after one year, I was like, "Holy crap — we've only been here a year!" Both of my parents worked for the same company for 30 years. I didn't think I would work at Freddie Mac my entire career, but at the same time leaving the company that quick was such a foreign concept to me. When I found out how much money my friends started making after switching companies, I said, "All right, well, then I'm going to leave and change companies too." Ever since then, having a friend to push me and say, "Why not? You know you can do that, so why shouldn't you be compensated so highly?" Having a friendly rivalry and someone to push you is key.

Brain Bucks — What a great idea here! We recommend HAVING A FRIEND (OR MENTOR) TO PUSH AND CHALLENGE YOU TO REACH NEW HEIGHTS AND CAREER GOALS. Friendly accountability can go a long way in ensuring you accomplish what you set out to do and that much more!

If you were 22 and just graduated from college, would you do anything differently to get to where you are now?

That's a tough question. There was one company I regret working for. That was a poor career choice on my part. Do more fact checking when you go for jobs — you have to know what you're going to be doing once you get the job. That's not always the case when you are right out of college because at that point you're just trying to get hired. It's step one — get hired and try to figure it out from there. But once you start moving and understanding what you can do and what your value-add is to an organization — it's really about describing your strengths in the interview process. The biggest thing now is when I'm talking to people on interviews, I'm not trying anymore — not trying to impress people, not trying to just say the right thing. What I am doing is saying what I want and what I can do. You have to be honest with yourself. Once you find out that you can add value, you have to be honest and go find what you want.

If I look for a position now, I can no longer look for a "good" position — I have to only look for the "perfect" position. That's the only way I can switch companies these days. My interviews used to be about saying the right thing, saying what they wanted to hear. Now I can go on an interview with a principal or director and say, "I know what I can bring to your company, what is your company going to bring to me and how is the company going to help me grow?"

Brain Bucks — What would he do differently? Perform more research on the companies you are interviewing with. This will decrease the chance that you accept a job offer with a company that is not a good match for you. Unfortunately, many people do not spend the time performing enough research. Also, know what your value is worth to a company in your industry. This will help ensure that you don't take a job opportunity where you are underpaid.

Were there any big challenges or obstacles you had to overcome to get to where you are now?

Complacency. My motto has always been "Always be comfortable, never be complacent." It really is tough and I think a lot of my friends have settled because they became complacent, hit a certain salary and said, "Well I'm comfortable living at that salary and I could try to hustle and do more," but decided that's where they want to be. For me, it's tough. With my last job, I went to work every day and received a huge paycheck. It was a good job with a very flexible and easy work arrangement — no Fridays, working from home when I wanted to, and I was being paid over $100,000. Leaving that job was so hard because I was literally signing myself up for more work, more responsibility and put myself out there in a pressure cooker. I knew if I stayed there any longer, I would never leave because it was so easy for me. I knew everyone and how to deal with them, influence them, get them to listen to me, but ultimately knew I had to move on or else I wasn't going anywhere else. I don't want to bad-mouth people who found their position or sweet spot — there is nothing wrong with staying. I just felt I hadn't hit my potential yet, and as a young single guy I felt I could take a risk.

Brain Bucks — Can you imagine leaving a job or position where you are comfortable and making over $100,000? The great John F. Kennedy once *said, "There are risks and costs to action. But they are far less than the long range risks of comfortable inaction."*

This quote perfectly sums up Michael's decision-making process. He knew he had it good in his current position. However, he realized that if he continued to stay at that particular job, he would be there for a very long time and not grow very much. The risk of action — finding a more challenging job — greatly outweighed the long-range risk of inaction — staying in the same position and not learning nor growing. To top it off, SINCE MICHAEL INTERVIEWED FOR OTHER JOBS WHILE HE HELD A CURRENT ONE, HE WAS STILL ABLE TO EARN A HIGHER SALARY WITH HIS NEXT COMPANY. Huge win for Michael!

Do you have any "aha" moments that stick out in your career so far?

Surprisingly yes. Right when I started, I entered into an 18-month rotational program — three jobs for six months each. That was part of the reason I chose the job offer out of school because I didn't know what I wanted to do but figured having options and exposure to different areas would help me ultimately find what it was I wanted to do. I started out doing production support. It was terrible, it wasn't fun, and I wasn't creating anything, which is important to me. Then I got placed on another project for my second rotation, which is when I went down the data migration path — which led into business intelligence which led into data architecture. At that moment, I could have either stayed at my position or moved into another position with the company but I told them, "I don't want to rotate to another position. I think this is a field that it is in demand and supply is completely short — I want to continue to do and learn more about this because I found what I want to do." I had to literally demand that I wasn't going to the third rotation, got my boss on board, and after some convincing, the company approved.

I imagine the company was thrilled to keep you where you wanted to be even as a first year employee after you demonstrated your value in that specific area.

Most definitely, we're the cheapest resources.

Did you have any mentors, heroes or career role models along your way?

I've talked to a lot different people about my career. One person I've always gone to and sought advice from was my cousin. He started out at Deloitte, then went to work for a small consulting company and now works at Microsoft. I knew he had gone through the consulting lifestyle. In starting my career, I could go to him because he knew a lot and was extremely successful. I would always use him as a sounding board as I made my career changes, so that was helpful. But it really is a different world in IT. When I left my fourth company for my fifth company, he was surprised as he was only on his third company over a much longer career compared to mine. But you have to be cognizant of the area you are in. A lot of people in IT and in this specific area jump around often. It was great advice when I started and I still talk to him about my career, but I have to make my own decisions a little more now.

Also, having my roommate being right there with me the entire time during my career has been amazing. Being in the same field, he and I have been very open about our salaries, jobs and decisions — it was never an awkward talk. He and I talking to each other has definitely helped me as well. If there's one thing I can re-emphasize, having that friendly rivalry and sounding board between two people headed in the same direction to speak to each other about career advice has been my biggest help throughout this whole process.

Brain Bucks — In our experience, having a mentor — ideally someone in a similar field who can share insight and lessons learned based on their experience is extremely helpful. Notice how Michael said earlier in his career, particularly when he was just out of college, he relied on his cousin as a sounding board — someone to bounce ideas and thought processes off of in order to make more informed decisions. This is essential to have in place no matter your job or career.

We caught up with Michael one year later to see if anything had changed since we last spoke.

Is there anything else you want to share with our readers?

I've now been with my current company for two years, the longest I've ever been working for with one company. The reason I've stayed so long is the growth opportunity of working for a small company — I actually see the benefit of the effort I put in, and also the flexibility of my current position in regards to my work-life balance. I hustled hard coming out of college, and while I can't point to any one thing that I missed, I've recently felt the lack of time spent on myself.

It was important to concentrate on my personal life for a period of time, and I was in a position that allowed me to do that. For me, that was traveling. I've spent a lot of time this year traveling the world. I was making enough to cover these trips while my company was OK with me taking personal time off to let me experience these trips without the worry about my finances or job back home.

I mentioned a motto I live by in our interview, "Always be comfortable, never be complacent." I stand by that, but I have an overarching motto now — "Do what makes you happy." A lot of people have judged me as someone who only cares about the dollars and cents that come with a job. The truth is, my compensation matters to me because it allows me to never say "no" to a new experience — no matter if that is travel, a night out or a new toy. But my positional flexibility is also an important part to those three things. I've turned down offers because I knew they would be 100-hour-per-week jobs and I wouldn't be enjoying life.

Not everyone knows what makes them happy right away, and that is completely fine. It is also something that changes over time. Some people love their jobs, while others use it as a means to an end. Being honest with yourself and your goals is the most important part of your career.

A Final Word

Well, there you have it. Perhaps you're thinking, "What should I do now?"

To start, we suggest you find your passion. Follow the blueprint to get internships. Work hard by providing more service and value for which you are paid. Create relationships and foster those relationships over time. Find a mentor and get personalized career advice. Build new skills and take on new projects. Follow our six insider secrets, and you will be on the road to increasing your income and earning potential in no time!

We didn't put notes pages in this book to simply take up space, so refer back to them and do it often. Take the advice, insights and strategies from those we interviewed in this book. Write down your goals and do what most people don't do with them — COME UP WITH A PLAN AND TAKE ACTION!

Finally, thank you for taking the time to read this book. We appreciate your interest and the investment you placed in yourself to become even more successful. YOU are the next generation of people who will lead and change the world!

We would love to hear your stories on your road to $100K as you advance in your career. Who knows — maybe we'll even have the opportunity to interview you someday for the next edition of this book!

If you feel this book was valuable and helped you in your career, we would love to read your review on our Amazon book page. At the same time, if there is anything we can do to improve or include in the next edition, we would love to hear from you as well. All stories and feedback can be sent to kev_and_wes@100Koutofcollege.com, and be sure to check out the website at www.100Koutofcollege.com for your FREE GIFT BONUSES!

Finally, as you have read through this book, you may have noticed it is full of quotes from some of the wisest, most successful and influential people in history. It would be only fitting to leave you with one more:

Create a definite plan for carrying out your desire and begin at once, whether you're ready or not, to put this plan into action.

—Napoleon Hill
American author & advisor to two United States Presidents

Appendix A – The Six Insider Secrets

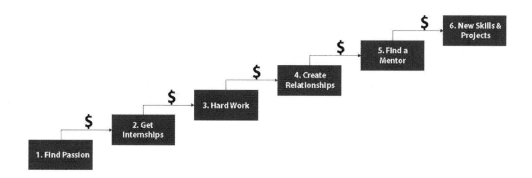

Appendix B — Top Paying Jobs & Industries

Job	Avg. Annual Pay	Projected Growth
Anesthesiologists	$246,320	18%
Surgeons	$240,440	18%
Oral and Maxillofacial Surgeons	$219,600	16%
Obstetricians and Gynecologists	$214,750	18%
Orthodontists	$201,030	16%
General Internists	$190,530	18%
Physicians and Surgeons	$189,760	18%
Family and General Practitioners	$186,320	18%
Psychiatrists	$182,700	18%
Chief Executives	$180,700	11%
Pediatricians (general)	$175,400	18%
Dentists (all other specialists)	$168,580	16%
Dentists	$166,810	16%
Nurse Anesthetists	$158,900	31%
Petroleum Engineers	$147,520	26%
Prosthodontists	$142,830	16%
Architectural/ Engineering Managers	$138,720	7%
Podiatrists	$137,480	23%
Marketing Managers	$137,400	12%
Natural Sciences Managers	$136,450	6%
Information System Managers	$136,280	15%
Lawyers	$133,470	10%
Airline Pilots / Engineers	$131,760	1%
Financial Managers	$130,230	9%
Law Professors	$126,270	19%
Sales Managers	$126,040	8%
Air Traffic Controllers	$118,780	1%
Compensation & Benefits Managers	$118,670	3%
Pharmacists	$118,470	14%
Physicists	$117,300	10%

The survey, which reflects May 2014 salary and employment data gathered from more than 1 million businesses. (**Source: Business Insider, May 2014**)

Appendix C — Highest Paying Jobs in 2015

Rank	Job	Annual Median Wage	Growth Outlook	Industry
1	Surgeon	$352,220	18%	Medical & Health Care
2	Psychiatrist	$181,880	18%	Medical & Health Care
3	Physician (*G.P.)	$180,180	18%	Medical & Health Care
4	Corporate Executive	$173,320	11%	Business & Technology
5	Dentist	$146,340	16%	Medical & Health Care
6	Petroleum Engineer	$130,050	26%	Engineering
7	Orthodontist	$129,110	16%	Medical & Health Care
8	Data Scientist	$124,150	15%	Business & Technology
9	Air Traffic Controller	$122,340	1%	Aviation
10	Pharmacist	$120,950	14%	Life Sciences

* G.P. = General Practice

Careers tracked by the 2015 Jobs Rated report, per U.S. Bureau of Labor Statistics data.

Source: Career Cast, 2015

Appendix D — Top 10 Highest-Paying Industries for Entry-Level Employees

Rank	Industry	Average Entry Level Pay
1	*Engineering	$77,500
2	Computer Programming	$75,000
3	Management Consulting	$65,000
4	Nursing	$55,000
5	Accounting	$52,000
6	Sales	$50,000
7	Financial Analyst	$47,000
8	Public Relations	$47,000
9	Graphic Design	$46,000
10	Copywriting	$41,000

*Engineering average entry-level salary taken from range of engineering specialties ($60,000–$95,000).

Source: cpJobs.com

Acknowledgements

This work is a product of many minds. We are grateful for the wisdom, insight and advice of many great thinkers who have influenced our careers and experience to make this all possible.

For the development and production of this book itself, we feel a deep sense of appreciation:

To our family, friends, teachers, professors, students and the companies who took a chance on us early in our careers to allow us to learn and grow while learning technologies, business and strategies along the way. To our mentors Dr. Jim Gilmour, James J. Quinlan, Gene O'Brien and Dave Olivieri, who were always in our corner giving us sound advice at pivotal points in our careers and still do today.

To our families who showed us how to live life with integrity and the true meaning of hustle and hard work.

To our coach David Braun of Wordflirt & yoogozi.com, who was instrumental in guiding us through brainstorming sessions on the content creation process for this book.

To Lou Redwood, Jonathan Turner, Chris Montrose, Tina Nelson, Zach Bedford, Joe Harper and Michael Freeman, who were kind enough to share their time, insight and career journeys with the readers through their enlightening interviews.

To Amy Keeler, Anthony Selbe, Brad White, Brendan Kelly, Brian Hawkins, Brian Myer, Bryan & Carrie Ercolano, Candy Manning, Christy Wilson, Cody Warren, Daniel Lopez, Dave Shaugnessey, Drew & Megan Amis, Erika Edwards, Frank DeMarco, Greg Raymond, Heather Perfetti, Jacob Gonzales Jacqueline Giordano, Jacqueline Waddle, Jason Robinson, Jen McGilloway, Jennifer Gordon, Joe Darhun, Joe McFarland, Jonathan Foucar-Szocki, Jonathon Zaremba, Katie Field, Katy Foucar-Szocki, Kevin Dupuis, Kevin

Luchko, Krista Bullock, Kyle Retallick, Michael Fitchko, Rich Slomka, Ranga Covindassamy, Raqule Branson, Rocky Arocho, Sean Carpenter, Sean Robinson, Shane O'Neill, Sonny Pastore, Stephanie Heiple, Stephen Boraske, Steve Price, Theepah Tharmalingam, Thomas Martin, TJ Colaeizzi, Tron Jones and Will Rinaldo for their key help with the launch of this project.

We thank you all.

About the Authors

Kevin Quinlan is a respected author, consultant, speaker and entrepreneur who has more than a decade of experience across the retail, consulting and education industries. As an independent consultant, he has spent over five years conducting data analysis on the career paths of thousands of executives from *Fortune 500* companies.

Kevin holds a bachelor's degree of *Business Administration* from James Madison University and a master's degree in *Business, Computer and Information Technology Education* from Temple University. He is also the Co-founder and President of the National Youth Mentor Academy, an organization that teaches students how to get into college and create a career of passion out of college.

In his free time, Kevin enjoys spending time with his family, traveling and playing golf. He currently volunteers as co-chair of the Economic Workforce and Development Committee for the Irvine Chamber of Commerce in Irvine, California, and as a wish granter with the Make-A-Wish Foundation.

Wes Rowlands is a recognized and successful author, businessman, speaker and entrepreneur. While earning his finance degree at Drexel University in Philadelphia, Wes held 10 internships with top financial institutions, including working on the floor of the stock exchange. This experience ultimately led him to his dream career on Wall Street.

After spending 11 years gaining industry experience, Wes decided to follow his passion and co-founded a company that helps families with college- and high school-age children plan for college and their careers.

In addition to running the company as CEO, Wes spends a portion of his time speaking to schools and institutions on topics such as leadership, career development, and finance. Delivering lectures to thousands of students, parents, teachers and executives, Wes has presented across the country, focusing on his passion of teaching students how to avoid the two biggest problems facing their generation today — student loan debt and no job! Wes is on a mission to help one student at a time to take responsibility and graduate into a successful future!

Notes

Notes

Notes

Notes

Notes

Notes

Notes

Notes

Notes

Notes

Notes

Notes

Notes

Notes

Notes

Made in the USA
San Bernardino, CA
23 February 2017